Daughter
OF THE
KING

POSSESSING YOUR
SPIRITUAL INHERITANCE

A. FRANCINE GREEN

Daughter of the King
POSSESSING YOUR SPIRITUAL INHERITANCE
A. FRANCINE GREEN

Published by:

⚙ LIFEWISE BOOKS

PO BOX 1072
Pinehurst, TX 77362
LifeWiseBooks.com

Interior Layout and Design | Yvonne Parks | PearCreative.ca

To contact the author:
BeyondChurchWalls.com

ISBN (Print): 978-1-947279-03-2
ISBN (E-book): 978-1-947279-04-9

Dedication

I am thankful for the prophetic voices of men and women of faith
who have touched my life over the years through their teachings,
books, and lifestyle of faith that encourage me to pursue and fulfill
God purposes for my life.

And to all my sisters in Christ who are chasing "*hard after Him.*"
May you rise to your fullest potential in Christ
on your way to your destiny!

Table of Contents

Acknowledgements

To my grandmother, Macy Pearl Brown, for laying a foundation of faith and grace in my life. Nothing on earth is like the love of a grandmother. She was the matriarch of our family. Macy is a female given name, which means "*weapon*" in Old French. My grandmother was a *weapon* in the hands of the Lord, protecting her family through prayer and righteous living. I was heartbroken when she passed away, because she was my rock. She wasn't a domineering woman, but she was powerful and helped to keep our family together during some tough times.

To my parents, Joseph and Doris Brown who've gone home to be with the Lord. I thank them for withstanding the onslaught of the enemy against the family many, many times, sticking it out until the end.

To my sons, Jonathan and Christopher: you have no idea how much I love you. What God has promised me He would do in your life! You've walked with me through the most challenging seasons of life and the most joyful. I praise God for what he is doing in your lives and for the men of God that you are becoming. I know you both have been called to do a mighty work in His Kingdom, and in due season you will walk into the destiny God has planned for you.

"You make known to me the path of life; you will fill me with joy in your presence, with eternal pleasures at your right hand."
Psalm 16:11

Introduction

GOD'S HIDDEN JEWELS

"And they shall be mine, saith the Lord of hosts,
in that day when I make up my jewels."
Malachi 3:17

Daughters, you are God's hidden jewels! You are His daughters, precious to Him, loved by Him. He has chosen you to be *"his treasured possession."*[1] Satan attempted to diminish our value as women, but God is redeeming and restoring women to His original purpose found in Genesis 1. We were created in His image to be *image bearers* and *carriers of His glory.*

It is a privilege and honor to write this book. I am neither a scholar nor a theologian. I don't have a degree in Biblical Studies. I'm just an ordinary woman who loves and chooses to obey her Heavenly Father. My love for Him, my relationship with Him, my willingness to serve, and my dependence upon the Holy Spirit make all the difference in my life. Never in my lifetime did I consider writing a book about anything, let alone about my spiritual journey. The year 1995 was a pivotal year in my life. My life drastically changed when I chose to submit my will to God's will. In 2004, the Lord spoke to me and told me I would write a book about my spiritual journey of faith. That was the furthest thing in my mind back then, with the many challenges I was facing. When I began to write, I heard the Spirit of the Lord say, *"I will bring all things to your remembrance I have taught you."*[2] Just like the disciples said in Acts 4:20: *"As for us, we cannot help speaking about what we have seen and heard"*, I cannot help but testify of what I have seen, heard, and experienced over the past 20 years and know there is more to come.

In this book, I share how the Lord bought me out of my personal *Egypt.* Egypt in the Bible can represent "a place of refuge and a place of oppression, a place to "come up out of" and a place to flee to."[3] I also share many of the truths I've learned from the Bible, as well as personal experiences, and wisdom from many courageous men and women that God the Father used along my journey towards pursuing the divine calling on my life.

With so many books already written about destiny and our identity in Christ, I felt inadequate to write such a book. I had the audacity to ask God, *"Why am I writing another book about our identity in Christ? Am I just echoing the same things others have already written?"*

In no way was I disrespecting the Heavenly Father. I'm thankful to have a relationship with Him that allows me to ask Him anything without reproach. As I obey Him, I know this is not just another book. It is God's desire for you to know Him. The Bible says, people are destroyed for a lack of knowledge.[4] They perish or go astray from the plans and purposes of God without vision. God wants to reveal Himself to you! He knows exactly how to get your attention. He can and desires to reveal Himself in many ways.

If you picked up this book based on the title, you've likely already questioned what God's purpose is for your life. You've probably read books, attended seminars and conferences, and taken courses seeking to know what God has purposed for you to do in the earth. But even after you've tried all those things, you still may be wondering "what is my purpose?" "When is it really going to happen for me?" I've asked those same questions myself. You may be serious about doing whatever it takes to find and fulfill your purpose, but up to this point, you haven't discovered God's plan for your life. What I hope and pray is that my faith journey will encourage you to pursue the plan God has for you at all cost.

This book is written to encourage and strengthen women from all walks of life to find their identity and purpose in Christ Jesus and pursue and fulfill His purpose for them in whatever sphere of influence He has assigned them.

I believe every one of us has a story to tell. Join me on a spiritual journey of faith as I share how God divinely orchestrated my steps to bring me to the place I am today. I have not arrived, but I *press toward the high calling of Christ.*[5]

Throughout history in the Old and New Testament, many women have made a difference in the Kingdom of God. Several women in particular have inspired me over the years. They were women who were obedient to God, exercised their faith, and rose above challenges to make a difference in their generation.

They were ordinary women called to do extraordinary things. Women such as Deborah, Ruth, Esther, and many more. Then there are lesser known women like Abigail, Hagar, and a certain woman mentioned in Luke 11:2—women of faith who made an impact on history. It's no coincidence that these women are spoken of in the Bible. Their stories and their lives help to influence our faith today.

In my personal journey, what I've learned from these women and their stories has helped to propel me toward fulfilling my God-given purpose. I hope to interweave their stories within my own to share how I have gleaned from their wisdom and faith to persevere along this journey.

They taught me to push beyond obstacles that could have ended my pursuit of the One who created me for His purposes.

Allow me to share with you a little about a few of these women. Let's begin with Eve, *Mother of All Living.*" Her story is one of the most famous in the Bible. Eve is the first women created by God in His image. She is the wife of Adam, and the mother of Cain and Abel. In Genesis 2:15-17, God plants a garden in Eden and puts the man (Adam) there to work the ground and keep it in order. He commands Adam, *"You are free to eat from any tree in the garden; but you must not eat from the tree of the knowledge of good and evil, for when you eat from it you will certainly die."* At that time, God had not created Eve. Then the Lord God says, *"It is not good for the man to be alone. I will make a helper suitable for him."*[6] Eve is deceived by Satan's lie, takes and eats some of the fruit from the tree of the knowledge of good and evil and gives some to Adam and he ate, they both disobeyed God and were expelled from the Garden. Thus, sin and deception entered the world. Enticement drew the man and the woman away from fellowship with the Father. What I admire about Eve is that she takes responsibility for her sin and tells the truth in Genesis 3:13.

Mary, the mother of Jesus, models an attitude of obedience and trust even when she doesn't fully understand God's plan to use her to bring forth His Son. An angel appears to her one day, announcing she has been chosen to give birth to Jesus.[7] Can you imagine that? An angel appearing to you telling you that you will have a child when you are not married, nor have you been with a man? Mary submits herself to God's will, and she faithfully follows Jesus from birth until His death on the cross. Even after the death of Jesus, she constantly prays with other believers for the Spirit in Jerusalem.

Esther's courage and wisdom are used by God to save His people from extinction. Esther is chosen by King Xerxes to be queen after Queen Vashti disobeys his orders.[8] After learning from her cousin Mordechai that the Jews are to be executed by Haman, she risks death by approaching the king with a request. Her deliverance of God's people is still celebrated by Jews today during the festival of Purim.

Mary Magdalene is a devoted follower of Jesus and supported Jesus' ministry financially. An encounter with Jesus' mercy and forgiveness transforms her life forever. Mary is one of the group of holy women who stand as near as they can during the crucifixion.[9] She is the first at the tomb to see the risen Lord, and she delivers the good news to the disciples about His resurrection. What an honor to be remembered as a committed follower of Christ.

These are just a few of the more notable women whose stories serve as an example to women everywhere. Satan has done much to exploit and degrade women, since that fatal day in the garden, by continuing to change God's truth into a lie to mislead women and keep them from their spiritual inheritance. But God has an eternal plan to restore the essence of a woman and use His daughters in these last days for His Kingdom purposes. I believe women will be a force to be reckoned with in this coming move of God. We can no longer sit back and allow Satan to destroy our families, our children, and our livelihood. Women everywhere are hearing the call of God, coming out of complacency, and taking back what the devil has attempted to steal from them.

God's hidden jewels have a deep love and adoration for Him; they have a reverential awe and profound respect of His majesty and authority. Many of God's daughters have faithfully served throughout the years with no apparent reward, but their service has not gone unnoticed. There is coming a day when He will act on your behalf. And that day has arrived!

ENDNOTES

Deuteronomy 7:6

John 14:26

Elwell, Walter A. 'Entry for Egypt" "Evangelical Dictionary of Theology" 1997, Bible Study Tools, Web. March 25, 2017, http://www.biblestudytools.com/dictionary/egypt/.Hosea 4:6

Philippians 3:14

Genesis 2:18

Luke 1:30-33

Esther 2:17

Luke 23:49

Chapter 1

AWAKEN THE DAWN

"The fact that I am a woman does not make me a different kind of Christian, but the fact that I'm a Christian does make me a different kind of woman."
Elisabeth Elliot[1]

God works everything out in agreement with the counsel and design of His own will. Not only is God's plan greater than you think, it is good. God's plan leads to a bright future now and forever. He wants us to know Him and to desire His plan and perfect will for our life. He waits for us to seek Him with expectant hearts, and He longs for that moment when we ask Him to show us the mysteries of His Kingdom.

God desires to bring His people into revelation knowledge of Him and the power of His resurrection. Revelation is imparted to you by the Spirit of God. We cannot understand the spiritual things apart from the Spirit of God. 1 Corinthians 2:12 says:

"What we have received is not the spirit of the world, but the Spirit who is from God, so that we may understand what God has freely given us. This is what we speak, not in words taught us by human wisdom, but in words taught by the Spirit, explaining spiritual realities with Spirit-taught words. The person without the Spirit does not accept the things that come from the Spirit of God, but considers them foolishness, and cannot understand them because they are discerned only through the Spirit."

You are more precious and valuable to God than you know. God was planning your salvation and deliverance before the world was even created. Because He loves you, He made plans to rescue you. *"I will protect you because you know my name. When you call to me, I will answer you. I will be with you when you are in trouble. I will save you and honor you. I will satisfy you with a long life. I will show you how I will save you."*[2]

God created us male and female to fulfill a specific purpose on the earth. It is important to understand who we are in Him before we can do what He has called us to do. The purpose is not just for your own personal benefit, but for His purposes and His mission--living God's purpose for His glory.

Awakened to New Life

In this book, I share my personal journey of faith, including painful family difficulties that taught me to look to God for answers when life wasn't so simple and the world's answers didn't work. There had to be another way. What I discovered is that God was in control and using those painful seasons to grow me into the woman He created me to be from the foundation of the world. My *"light and momentary troubles"* were achieving *"an eternal glory that far outweighs them all."* [3]

I began a spiritual journey that changed my perspective of life forever. I embarked on this journey with no understanding of where it would lead me. The journey evolved into an awakening of my soul, which led me to a place of wholeness and freedom in Christ. The journey was toward Christlikeness, a natural progression of transformation, wholeness, and growing in my understanding of our Heavenly Father and my true identity in Christ. This journey was filled with growing pains and faith challenges, but led to a deeper knowledge of God's will and His ways through study of His Word, daily conversations with Him through prayer, and learning to give up control and trust Him with my life. Many times, I cried out for His wisdom, insight and understanding as He shielded me and guarded my course.

When God truly begins to move in your life, it exposes areas that need restoration, repair, and rebuilding. My hope was to resolve the marital challenges I was facing at the time, but God had other plans in mind. My secure little world was now being uprooted and torn apart. Isn't that what He says in Jeremiah 1:10? There were old thought patterns and ways that had to be uprooted and torn down. Fallow (uncultivated, barren) ground needed to be broken up so that He could build and *"plant the good seeds of righteousness"* in my heart to be able to *"harvest a crop of love"* until He comes and *"shower[s] righteousness upon me."*[4] The expression, "Break up your fallow ground" means, break off all your wicked habits; clear your hearts of weeds, in order that they may be prepared for the seed of righteousness, and the good seed of the Word will have room to grow and bear fruit for God's Kingdom.

I was about to enter a realm—a kingdom—I knew nothing about. But once I got a taste of God's goodness, I was on a quest to discover my true identity and serve wholeheartedly in His Kingdom. As I began to pursue Him, I realized that there had to be more. I was hungry for His presence in my life. I'm not satisfied with just knowing about Him. I want to know Him and *"the power of His resurrection"*.[5]

I realized I was spiritually dead. Ephesians 2:1 states that, *"before we knew Christ, we were dead in transgressions and sins.*" Because of Adam's sin, which we inherited, we are all separated from God, who is life. We cannot experience, understand, or relate to a holy and perfect God in our unregenerate state, nor can we enter His kingdom.

Our need for spiritual awakening is great: "*The god of this age has blinded the minds of unbelievers, so that they cannot see the light of the gospel that displays the glory of Christ.*"[6] We must be roused from our dead state and made alive in Christ; we must be "*awakened*" spiritually, or, as Jesus put it, we must be "*born again*" or "*born of water and the Spirit*" to enter the Kingdom of God.[7]

Once we accept Christ as our Savior, we are not expected to achieve instant spiritual maturity. Rather, the Christian life is a process involving both our openness to receive Him as our personal Lord and Savior and God's work in us.

God uses the events in our lives to shape us, to teach us, and to grow us. I started this pursuit becoming like a child, seeing the world through naïve eyes, influenced by the flesh, and in need of basic teaching about God, Jesus Christ, the Holy Spirit, and my position in Christ. I recall after hearing the Word of God preached consistently and studying Scriptures, I thought to myself "I'm so smart, I'm dumb." Why did I think this? Because I had worldly knowledge, yet I'd never been trained in the ways of God. We must do more than hear the Word and say, "that's a good word." We must process that Word in cooperation with the Holy Spirit to bear fruit in our lives. When God changes our lives, then He can change other people's lives through us.

How It All Began

I'd like to share with you a little more about my story and how it all began. Did anything significant or world-changing happen the day I was born? Maybe, maybe not, yet there were many events that impacted our nation during that time. Nineteen fifty-seven was the peak of the Baby Boomer years. Dr. Martin Luther King Jr. was spearheading a nationwide resistance to racial segregation and discrimination in the U.S. Federal Troops were sent to Arkansas to enforce anti-segregation laws; Toyota started selling cars in the U.S.; the Soviet Union launched the first space satellite Sputnik 1, and Elvis Presley purchased Graceland.[8] The popular toys were slinkies and hula hoops. Oh my! Some of you may be wondering "what in the world is a slinky?"

When segregation ended and schools were integrated, my parents decided to send me and my siblings to a predominantly "white" school during a time when being "black" or "Negro" wasn't popular, and you were sure to be called the "N" word at least once. Since then, I've come to understand that was a part of God's plan for me. I was a little eight-year-old girl alone in a sea of unfriendly faces, who by the grace of God sat quietly in a classroom where she felt unwelcomed. When I look back over the early years of my childhood, I can now see how God was prophetically preparing for this time.

Who would have ever thought that God could take a small-town girl and transform her life by grace to become *"a servant of this gospel by the gift of God's grace given me through the working of his power."*[9]

Growing into Adulthood

I grew up in a county located in the Commonwealth of Virginia, a short distance away from the state's capital. After graduating from high school, I went on to a Historically Black College (HBCU) in Virginia. After graduating from college, I worked in my field of study for a short time until I eventually decided to return to school and obtain a degree in information systems. I was searching for the "American Dream," and the prospects of having a promising career and quality of life were favorable in that field of study. While working on my degree, I interned with the State of Virginia Information System Audit Division. The staff embraced me in such a way that it opened doors for me to work in the IT Audit industry before graduating from the program. Eventually, I was offered a position with the audit department at the local university I was attending. Awesome! I had no idea it was a divine setup that would position me in the direction God wanted me to go.

Although things were going well, I had this longing within my heart/spirit that I did not understand. I had a desire to move to the Washington, DC Metropolitan area, also known as the DMV, even though I didn't know anyone or had little familiarity with the area. I was clueless—not rich, a shopaholic, or socially successful, like the girls in the movie "Clueless," but simply unaware of what life would be like if I made this transition. So why in the world would a young single woman want to move to an area she had only visited a few times, let alone consider living there when she was doing well? What I didn't know is that it was a silent longing deposited in me by my Heavenly Father that I had no knowledge would manifest later in my life.

I came to appreciate that God was always pursuing me. When I look back, I can see how through life circumstances, He was wooing me to an unknown place. *"But now I am going to woo her – I will bring her out to the desert and I will speak to her heart."*[10] God draws and woos us because He is jealous for our love. He delights in alluring us and revealing Himself to those who wholeheartedly seek Him.

In 1990, I married a man whose family just so happen to live in Maryland right across the District of Columbia line. Things that make you go hmm…right? Talk about divine orchestration. One day my then husband and I decided to move from Virginia to Maryland so we could pursue a better life. This was a major transition for both of us because we were accustomed to life in a smaller city or town. I had no idea that God had a totally different plan for my life. Thinking back, only my Heavenly Father could have orchestrated something like this and put me on the inescapable path towards destiny. Psalm 37:23 says, He orders our steps and delights in every detail of our lives. Since that time, I have experienced many divinely orchestrated events that positioned me for His purposes.

It appeared as though God wanted me to move there to have a successful career. Now, I believe He led me into the wilderness, an unknown place, far away from my support network of family and friends and everything that I knew and was comfortable with to set me on the path He ordained. But during those wilderness years of waiting, longing, and crying, I experienced God *"speaking tenderly"* to me, reminding me of His presence, that only He and not success or career advancement would truly satisfy me.

As I reflect more on my journey and listen to the story of others, it seems that God does this quite a bit: from my perspective, He *"lures"* us into doing something or going somewhere under the pretense of fulfilling our personal desires, and then when we get there, we find He has much deeper purposes in store for us.

My Personal Awakening

My personal awakening came during a tumultuous time in my life when I was going through a difficult marriage. We were at the point of separation/divorce until my ex-husband and I were introduced to a deliverance ministry that helped men and women with drug addiction and other life challenges.

When everything fell apart, I found myself in a place of brokenness. Although I was broken emotionally and spiritually bankrupted at the time, I saw broken individuals and families whose lives had been shattered by addiction. I heard stories of pain and disappointment that challenged me to look at life from a different set of lenses. I was compelled by compassion to set aside my own pain to help in any way I could.

As I matured in my faith, I understood that Jesus loved people and was moved with compassion to help them. Compassion is not merely sympathy, or an emotional response to a need. When moved with real compassion, we respond to a need with action. My heart's desire was to align my motivations with His and come alongside Him in what He was doing to restore broken lives. The harvest was plentiful, yet the laborers were few. The Lord gradually began to send laborers into the harvest. God moved mightily during those days. We saw many people saved, set free from a life of sin and addiction, families restored, and many people called into ministry. Zechariah 9:16 says, "*The Lord, their God will save his people on that day as a shepherd saves his flock. They will sparkle in his hand like jewels in a crown.*"

All of this left a deep impression on my life. I am passionate about sharing God's heart for people. My motivation for what I do flows out of a heart to serve and glorify God and not myself.

Transformed by Grace

> "*We were therefore buried with him through baptism into death in order that, just as Christ was raised from the dead through the glory of the Father, we too may live a new life.*" – Romans 6:4

God's grace can radically transform lives. Because of Christ's death and resurrection, we can walk in newness of life. In essence, the old sin nature is dead and buried, and now we are able to walk in this new life God has given us by grace. We are transformed into a new creation in Christ, reborn, made holy and blameless before our Creator.

What does it mean to walk in newness of life? The Apostle Paul put it this way: "Therefore, if anyone is in Christ, the new creation has come: The old has gone, the new is here."[11] To walk in newness of life requires us to abandon our old sinful ways and walk according to the Spirit. "So, I say, walk by the Spirit, and you will not gratify the desires of the flesh."[12]

No matter who you are or what you have done in the past, the blood of Jesus can cover it. He can make all things new. At our conversion, we entered into a covenant with God through the blood of Jesus. Hebrews 10:17 says, "Their sins and lawless acts I will remember no more." When you can grasp all that God has done to restore you to Himself, it inspires you to make true life changes.

A Radical Life in Christ

Christianity is not just a religion, it's a way of life. It's a lifestyle of faith. You have faith in the One that you cannot see with your natural eyes, but you know He exist by the things that He made. The truth is, we are surrounded by evidence of a Creator who is wise, powerful, and loving. Life in the Spirit is an indescribable adventure with God. Your life will never be the same!

In making this transition, what would this new lifestyle actually look like? Would it mean leaving behind security, money, convenience, even family for Him? Abandoning everything for the sake of the gospel? Taking up the cross daily? Yes. That's what it meant for me. It may seem a little radical to some, but it has been one of the best decisions I ever made in life.

By definition Christianity is the religion based on the person and teachings of Jesus, or its beliefs and practices,[13] but when we choose a spirit-led life of faith in an invisible God, Christianity becomes so much more. It becomes confidence in Him and His Word. It becomes a life of passion. And as God's children, we become who we are through relationship with an invisible God. As Bill Johnson, Senior Pastor of Bethel Church in Redding, California says, "*Christianity was never meant to be a life of disciplines. It was always meant to be a life of passion."*[14]

Part of living a spirit-led life is learning to accurately discern the leading of the Holy Spirit. This may be one of the greatest challenges we can face as Christians. Learning to abide (remain) in the Lord and maintain a living relationship with Him begins with hearing and obeying His Word. God told Israel to obey His written Word and His voice. He gives us the same command today. *"Obey me and I will be your God and you will be my people. Walk in obedience to all I command you, that it may go well with you."*[15]

The same applies to us today as we seek the leading of the Holy Spirit. By studying the Word and meditating on it, the mind is renewed to spiritual things. Renewing the mind is an important and necessary part in hearing the Spirit of God. *"The person without the Spirit does not accept the things that come from the Spirit of God but considers them foolishness, and cannot understand them because they are discerned only through the Spirit."*[16]

God speaks to us in many ways such as: His Word, the Holy Spirit, a still small voice or a whisper, wise counsel, our circumstances and thoughts. God can also speak through nature, His creation, music, dreams and visions, and supernatural manifestations. The Lord constantly speaks to us providing His direction. Jesus tells us that His sheep hear His voice, and they will never follow the voice of a stranger.[17]

You must learn to clearly distinguish God's voice and obey His commands. Instead of going through life blindly, you can ask for the wisdom of God to guide and protect you. Learning to hear His voice is invaluable. My life was radically transformed by hearing the voice of the Lord.

As a minister, I depend on God's Spirit to give me direction. I learned to rely on the inner promptings of the Holy Spirit and to be sensitive to His leadings. Hearing God's voice is one of the most important factors in developing spiritually, and fulfilling His purposes.

The Spirit and the Word will always agree. You can be certain that the Spirit will never lead you into doing something that is opposite of God's written Word. The Spirit guides you to truth.

Motivation for Real Change

Change is difficult. We must be motivated to change, otherwise we remain stagnant in our spiritual walk. Have you ever tried to start a new routine like a diet or fitness program, only to feel frustrated after just a few days because your commitment got sidetracked? I know I have many times.

Change is a process. We may try to change for the better by only dealing with our behavior instead of the real issues, but the truth is that a superficial focus only leads to superficial change. Or, if we're primarily motivated to change in order to meet our own personal, short-term gains, we won't experience lasting change either. We must have the courage and desire to face the truth about ourselves and our lives, instead of running from it. We must be motivated to seek God's will and not our own.

We are expected to grow into mature believers. No one likes to be described as "immature." God is more concerned about inwardly transforming you to become more like Christ. And this type of change doesn't come by faking it until you make it or by trying harder. Real change begins with transforming how you think and believe so you can come to the point of accepting how deeply you are loved. When you know the depth of His love, you will strive to change *"being confident of this, that he who began a good work in you will carry it on to completion until the day of Christ Jesus."* [18]

Renew Your Mind, Renew Your Life

Sometimes I think too much. I think of what I can do more, what should have been and could have been. A friend of mine tells me that I overanalyze everything. Maybe I do? The good news is that I have an opportunity to do something about all the thoughts that are not well-pleasing to God, before they enter my heart and become a part of me!

Changing your thinking will transform your life. What we think about is crucial to who we are. Who we are is shaped by the thoughts we choose to let into our mind and heart. The truth is, we cannot have a positive, productive life and have a negative mind. One of the most important steps we can take toward achieving our greatest potential in life is to learn to monitor our thoughts and their impact on our attitude. We must learn to control the thoughts and keep negative thoughts from entering our hearts. Proverbs 23:7 says, *"Be careful how you think; your life is shaped by your thoughts."*[19] I can truly attest to this. I can now think back to times when I didn't control my thoughts, and my attitude was less than perfect which was reflected outwardly in words and actions.

Our minds can be a battlefield. The enemy of our soul bombards our mind with cleverly devised nagging thoughts, suspicions, doubts, fears, questions, and theories. Satan tells us things about ourselves, other people and, circumstances that are just not true. Remember how he deceived Adam and Eve? Jesus says, *"he is a liar and the father of lies."*[20]

When wrong thoughts are established, we must renew our minds in agreement with God's Word. We need to battle unseen forces to keep our thoughts pure. As we go through the day, we can seize thoughts and attitudes that are contrary to God's will and His Word and keep them from gaining control of our mind and heart. God has provided a way for us to overcome negative, unhealthy thoughts. It's a matter of changing our thinking to His way. When negative or wrong thoughts creep into our minds, we need to give them over to Jesus. Every argument and pretension that sets itself up against the knowledge of God, we can *"take captive to make it obedient to Christ."*[21]

Proverbs 23:7 tells us, *"for as he thinks in his heart so is he."*[22] The word "thinks" here indicates we are whatever we believe about ourselves. The truth is, what we think on is what we believe and, in time, what we become. Our thought lives lead to what will play out in our lives personally, emotionally, and spiritually, and will even influence how we step into God's plan for our lives.

Satan attempts to set up strongholds in our minds. A stronghold is a mental disagreement you believe that contradicts the person and power of Christ and the Word of God. A stronghold is a fortress of arguments designed to take your mind captive and hold you prisoner. They are lies the enemy tells you that keep the Word of God from dominating your thought life and hinder the sanctifying work of God in your life. Here are just a few of the lies Satan perpetrates to keep you in the darkness:

- Lies or untruths you tell yourself: I have to be perfect. I must be happy. I need people to agree with me. I cannot shake my past. I deserve better than this.
- Lies or untruths the world tells you: I must be true to myself. I am number one. I am only human; everybody makes mistakes. This may be a true statement. We all stumble in many ways, just don't allow your mistakes to become an excuse and stop you from maturing in the truth of God's Word. John 8:32 says, "Then you will know the truth, and the truth will set you free."
- Lies or untruths that distort the truth of the Gospel: Does God really love me? Does He really hear me? Will He heal me?

What consumes your mind, controls your life. What you decide to obsess over in your mind, ruminating, reviewing, and rewinding over and over, will ultimately be what controls you. So how can we control the thousands of thoughts that enter our mind each day? How do we take our thoughts captive? We need to have the mind of Christ activated in our lives. As we get to know God through prayer, scriptures, and relationship, God's thoughts become more active, and pretty soon those negative thoughts begin to diminish.

Take any negative thought captive. Confront your negative thoughts each time they pop into your mind. Choose to focus your thoughts on the right things. Think about those things that are *"true, noble, right, pure, lovely, and admirable,"* and *anything that is "excellent or praiseworthy."*[23]

When an army moves in a battle, they destroy the fortress and then take captives. As believers, we take captive every thought that exalts itself against the knowledge of Christ by destroying the fortresses that have been set up in our minds. By the Holy Spirit, we can receive grace and power to bring our thoughts into captivity, and in this process, we become transformed into the person God wants us to be.

Living When Dying Is Gain

Paul says in Philippians 1:21, *"For me, to live is Christ and to die is gain."* At the time, Paul is in prison in the city of Rome, facing trial, knowing he is going to be executed for his faith in Christ.

What does it mean "to live is Christ?" Jesus tells us to die to ourselves so that He can become the center of our lives. In Matthew 10:39, Jesus clearly acknowledges that following Him involves risking the safety, security, and satisfaction we find in the world. But in the end, following Jesus leads to a radical reward that this world could never offer.

You must come to the end of yourself before you can truly live for God. To do this, I had to reckon myself dead from sin and ask myself if the reward found in Him is worth the risk of my following Him at all costs. The Lord spoke to me once at a time when I was being challenged in my faith, and asked whether I would follow Him "even if it looked like I was being deceived." The answer was a resounding "Yes."

Idolatry is putting anything other than God at the center of your life. It could be family, children, relationships, or your job. What was God's first commandment to His people? Not to have anything other than God at the center of their lives and not to love anything or anyone more than they love Him.

When you think about idols, you may think of TV shows like *"American Idol," "Dancing with the Stars,"* or reality TV celebrities who capture the world's attention on a weekly basis. Simply put, an idol is valuing something more than God or placing something or someone other than God at the center of our lives. What are some of your idols? What do you worry about most? What preoccupies you the most? What do you daydream about? Where do you fixate your thoughts? Thinking about those questions helps determine what drives you and keeps you from giving God first place in your life.

One Spiritual Lesson We Need to Learn

One of my first spiritual lessons involved learning how to cultivate the fruit of the spirit in my life. Specifically, I needed to cultivate patience and self-control when I started my walk with the Lord. I had to trust the Holy Spirit to help me tame my tongue, or keep my mouth shut and allow the Holy Spirit to rule. Otherwise, the course of my life and my children's lives would have been set aflame. Or better yet, our whole lives would have been turned into a blazing flame of chaos and destruction. It would have been like pouring gasoline on an already unstable situation. James 3:6 says, *"The tongue also is a fire, a world of evil among the parts of the body. It corrupts the whole body, sets the whole course of one's life on fire, and is itself set on fire by hell."*

How often do we open our mouths thinking that we have a right to say whatever we want, but have no idea the damage that can be caused by an unruly, careless tongue? James 1:26 says if we consider ourselves religious, but don't keep a tight rein on our tongues, we deceive ourselves and our religion is worthless. Ouch. How many Christian marriages and relationships are splintered by a loose tongue? We must gain control of our tongue before our lives are destroyed by it.

Sometimes we say or do things on impulse, only to realize that what we have said or done does not measure up to the fruit of the Spirit. That quickening of our spirit, that regret, is part of the work of the Holy Spirit guiding us into the truth. At that moment, we may ask God's forgiveness for our misstep and ask for the Spirit's help to work on our words or actions.

On the positive side, as we live from day to day in tune with the Holy Spirit, He will lead us and help us grow the fruit of the Spirit. It requires the Holy Spirit help to produce the fruit with our participation and continual efforts to develop them in our lives.

Paul wrote in Ephesians 5:18, *"Be filled with the Spirit."* Let the filling of the Spirit be more than a one-time event, but a continual infilling we can be intentional about. Even though we are involved in many things during the day, we may consciously reach out to the Lord and seek the help of the Holy Spirit in a moment of time.

Romans 8:14 says, *"For those who are led by the Spirit of God are the children of God."* In verse 16, Paul reveals one special way the Holy Spirit leads us. *"The Spirit himself testifies with our spirit that we are God's children."* That witness of the Spirit to our spirit assures us of our relationship with the Holy Spirit.

God's Will vs My Will

> *"I am the vine; you are the branches. If you remain in me and I in you, you will bear much fruit; apart from me you can do nothing." – John 15:15*

You will have times throughout your life that you will want to respond to situations based on your own wisdom and understanding. I can honestly tell you this approach will get you in trouble. When it comes to discerning God's will, you should always go to the Bible and ask the Holy Spirit to reveal God's will for your life or His will for whatever situation you may be facing. Find out what God has to say and make your decisions based on biblical truths and the leading of the Spirit. Look to see how God generally does things throughout Scriptures, and how He has consistently related to people throughout history. You can expect Him to work in a similar way with you. Don't turn to solutions, programs, and methods that falsely appear to be answers to spiritual problems.

Once you know the will of God, you can adjust your life to Him. The focus needs to be on what God is doing, and not on your own life. Jesus is our perfect example. Jesus said in John 6:38, "*For I have come down from heaven not to do my will but to do the will of him who sent me.*" Jesus completed every assignment the Father gave Him.

God reveals His will in numerous ways. God speaks by the Holy Spirit through the Bible, prayer, circumstances, and the Church to reveal Himself, His purposes, and His ways. What I've learned is that often, God asks us to make the choice to do His will before we know the specific details of His plan. That's because part of God's plan is to develop in us a trust of His love, character and His kindness towards us.

I decided to turn my life and my will over to His care many years ago, to be "*crucified with Christ*" so that "*Christ lives in me.*"[24] The life I now live, I live by faith in the Son of God. This may seem more radical than most Christians are willing to do. I'm sure that some who know me personally would agree. "Good religious people" can remain partially submitted to God (which really means not submitted to God) for years with the assumption that they are living by faith.

Yet, we are to seek His will and His ways first above all else. That's what I chose to do. Now I'm reaping the fruit of that choice.

Jesus demonstrated His loyalty and obedience to God and to the Word when He was led into the wilderness by the devil. He was tested, and then returned in the power of the Spirit to operate in the anointing, bringing salvation for many sons and daughters.

Jesus submitted Himself to God's will, suffered hardship, but overcame and now is at the right hand of the Father making intercession for us making it possible for us to live in obedience to God's will.

Work in Progress

Too many of God's children are living below our privilege and short of what Christ died for us to have. I sometimes hear people say, "I'm a work in progress," "God's still working on me," or "God knows my heart." All of that may be true. Yet, when I hear those phrases, I cringe in my spirit. We should never allow being a "work in progress" to become an excuse for not maturing in Christ. In some cases, what we are saying is "I'm not ready to change that area of my life." Just like our natural parents, God's desire is that we grow into mature sons and daughters. We are "*God's handiwork*" or "*God's workmanship*."[25] We were created for more.

Don't get me wrong. I'm not saying that everyone uses this as a reason not to change. Many people struggle to change because they are trying to do it in their own power. Even the apostle Paul struggled at one point in time, but he realized he could not do it on his own. That's why he said in Romans 7:15-20:

> "*I do not understand what I do. For what I want to do I do not do, but what I hate I do. And if I do what I do not want to do, I agree that the law is good. As it is, it is no longer I myself who do it, but it is sin living in me. For I know that good itself does not*

dwell in me, that is, in my sinful nature. For I have the desire to do what is good, but I cannot carry it out. For I do not do the good I want to do, but the evil I do not want to do—this I keep on doing. Now if I do what I do not want to do, it is no longer I who do it, but it is sin living in me that does it."

Although he wanted to do good, evil was right there with him. Paul understood his deliverance came through Jesus Christ.

God has a wonderful plan for our lives, but we must grow and mature into sonship. The faith we have, our new life in Christ, the child of God we have become is God's work, not ours. *"God made us alive with Christ."*[26]

ENDNOTES

1. Elliot, Elizabeth. "A quote by Elisabeth Elliot," *Goodreads*, Web. March 25, 2017, http://www.goodreads.com/quotes/112770-the-fact-that-i-am-a-woman-does-not-make.
2. Psalm 91:14-16 God's Word Translation (GWT)
3. 2 Corinthians 4:17
4. Hosea 10:12
5. Philippians 3:10
6. 2 Corinthians 4:4
7. John 3:3-8
8. Pearson, Steve. "What Happened in 1957 Important News and Events, Key Technology and Popular Culture" *The People History*, Web. March 25, 2017, http://www.thepeoplehistory.com/1957.html.
9. Ephesians 3:7
10. Hosea 10:12
11. 2 Corinthians 4:4
12. Galatians 5:16
13. "Christianity". *Dictionary.com* Unabridged. Random House, Inc. Web. 25 March. 2017. http://www.dictionary.com/browse/christianity.
14. Johnson, Beni, Johnson, Bill, Silk, Danny, Vallotton, Kris, Dedmon, Kevin, Liebscher, Banning, "*Spiritual Java*" (Shippensburg, PA: Destiny Image Publishers, 2010), March 26, 2017. 240.
15. Jeremiah 7:23
16. 1 Corinthians 2:14
17. John 10:3-5
18. Philippians 1:16
19. Proverbs 23:7 GNT
20. John 8:44
21. 2 Corinthians 10:4-5
22. Proverbs 23:7 KJV
23. Philippians 4:8
24. Galatians 2:20
25. Ephesians 2:10
26. Ephesians 2:5

Chapter 2

GOD'S DIVINE CREATION

"Then God said, 'Let us make mankind in our image, in our likeness, so that they may rule over the fish in the sea and the birds in the sky, over the livestock and all the wild animals, and over all the creatures that move along the ground."
Genesis 1:26

What does it mean to be created in God's image? The Hebrew root for image of God is *tselem Elohim,*[1] which means image, shadow or likeness of God. You are a snapshot or facsimile of God. As children of God made in His image, we are people of destiny. We are destined to be overcomers to the praise and glory of God.

"So God created mankind in his own image, in the image of God he created them; male and female he created them." [2] Being created male and female does not mean women have lesser value than men. We have been created equal. The term equal means likeness or sameness in quality. As children

of God, we have been created in the Father's likeness, having the same or similar qualities and characteristics as Him, yet we are unique.

Women were created with unique feminine characteristics when God made the first woman, Eve. We are God's prize possession, created a little lower than the angels. Crowned with glory and honor.[3] He knows the intimate details of our lives, including the number of hairs on our heads and we are worth more than many sparrows.[4]

I Am Fearfully and Wonderfully Made

You, my dear sister, are precious, priceless, and loved by an amazing God in Heaven. You are fearfully and wonderfully made. You are not an accident. You are not a mistake. God created you the way you are for a reason. You don't have to feel undue pressure to be like other people because God didn't make you like other people. You were created for His glory.

You were created intentionally for a divine purpose. It's no strange thing that you were placed strategically where you are at this time. You have been called by His own glory and goodness. His divine power has given you everything you need to accomplish your purpose in Him.[5]

God Created You Uniquely

Your identity is not wrapped up in some else's identity. Each one of us is unique and intricately put together by God. Many women are conscious of their bodies and outward image. Know this, God made all the delicate, inner parts of your body and knitted you together in your mother's womb. He made you wonderfully complex. And that's not a bad thing. His thoughts towards you are precious because He loves you. You cannot number nor count how often He thinks about you. You are God's pride and joy, the jewel of all creation. You are on His mind constantly.

Your days are also planned out ahead of time. King David was in awe of how God had created him. He says, *"For you created my inmost being; you knit me together in my mother's womb. I praise you because I am fearfully and wonderfully made; your works are wonderful, I know that full well."* [6]

God purposefully created you the way you are. You are a genuine and unique work of art produced by the Master. He saw your unformed body even before ultrasound imaging became available, and recorded every day of your life in His book. Isn't it amazing to know God recorded you in His book? He has every chapter of your life planned out. Your entire life was mapped out prior to your birth. It is up to you to walk the path He has laid out for you. I can promise that if He has written your life story, it is going to be good.

Maybe when you think about the kind of person you are, words like "average" or "not bad" come to mind. Sometimes you might see yourself as above average, but there are days when a closer look reveals insecurities and flaws that you can't ignore. If you ever consider yourself unremarkable or even ordinary, you're not seeing yourself in light of God's divine creation. When we discover the truth that we are God's unique design, it is overwhelming.

He knows your name, He sees your life, and He cares about the inner desires of your heart. God doesn't see as man sees. He can see things about you that no one else can see. Deep things. Hidden things, including those inner thoughts and desires that your family and friends have no idea are even floating around in your heart and mind. *"The LORD does not look at the things people look at. People look at the outward appearance, but the LORD looks at the heart."* [7]

Maybe you are a woman living in the "world" and have not accepted the gift of salvation given to all who believe in Christ. If that is you, ask Jesus to come into your heart and forgive you of your sins.[8] He will make you a new creature in Christ.

Or maybe you are a Christian who is going through life shackled in chains of addictions, feelings of shame, fear, hurt or unforgiveness, etc. God doesn't want you bound in chains. He wants to break every chain that binds you. Jesus came to set you free from captivity and to give you a full life. Christ wants to set you free!

It's also important that we teach and instill in our sons and daughters these spiritual truths at an early age to help them understand and embrace how God created them.

You, my dear sister, are fearfully and wonderfully made.

Fashioned by Love and Grace

> *"The one who has fashioned us for this very purpose is God, who has given us the Spirit as a deposit, guaranteeing what is to come."*
> – *2 Corinthians 5:5*

In our society, fashion is defined as a popular trend, especially in styles of dress and adornment or manners of behavior. We all love fashion and usually can't wait until the next season's styles are revealed. But did you know your days and life are fashioned by God the Master Designer before you were born? You are a Designer Original. A woman fashioned by God may not be perfect, but she is priceless. Even though I love to dress in the latest vogue, I would rather be fashioned by God's grace.

Know this, what man (mankind) rejects, God has designed as part of His perfect plan for you. Some of you may be dissatisfied with your outward appearance or abilities because you are looking at life from the perspective of human nature instead of eternity. The apostle Paul grieved over a physical defect that caused him embarrassment. He felt it was a hindrance to his work and prayed three times for God to take it away. The answer the Lord gave him was, *"My grace is sufficient for you, for my power is made perfect in weakness."*[9] Can you imagine, even Paul was concerned about a defect he felt may cause people to reject him? Once the apostle determined to live by God's strength, he found that his weakness became an asset to his life and began rejoicing in it. No matter what defect we may have, God's strength is made perfect in our weakness.

What you may think is a weakness may actually be God's blessing. When Paul understood that God's grace was sufficient, he delighted in his weaknesses, in insults, in hardships, in persecutions and in difficulties because he learned that there is power in weakness. In the areas where you fall short, God's grace is sufficient. And His strength exceeds anything you can do for yourself. Or anything you can do for God.

Your days were fashioned as was your life. If you walk by His leading, you will experience the joy of the journey in every circumstance, and you'll have the delight of what awaits at the end of this journey.

True Beauty Unveiled

> *"The unfading beauty of a gentle and quiet spirit, which is of great worth in God's sight." – 1 Peter 3:4*

When I was younger, I loved fashion and would spend time reading women's magazines like *Seventeen*, *Vogue*, and *Glamour* when possible. I flowed with the cultural trends of the day. I still love fashion and shoes, yet as I grew older, my interest for reading fashion magazines eventually faded. As my values changed, these magazines no longer matched my moral beliefs or God's view of women.

Today, many of these magazines are a little racier in content. We're bombarded daily with messages and choices about what to wear, celebrity lives, relationships, and relationship breakups along with health, beauty, and hairstyles. And not only magazines, but the Internet and social media. What I've noticed is how the lines are blurred between what's appropriate for women, young adults, and young teens. It seems anything goes. The Lord is calling His daughters to arise and come away with Him. In Song of Solomon 2:2 it reads, "As a lily among brambles, so is my love among the young women." God loves His daughters so much. We should long to hear His voice speaking to us, guiding us, and leading us along the path He has chosen.

"My beloved spoke and said to me, 'Arise, my darling, my beautiful one, come with me.'" – Song of Solomon 2:10

I love being feminine. I love dressing up, donning high heels, and wearing makeup and perfume. I love to encourage, nurture, and add value to others I encounter. I love encouraging women of all ages, shapes, and sizes to embrace their true beauty from the inside out. Women should embrace the true beauty that they are!

Women have lived for a long time under the pressure to be beautiful outwardly. Yet many women haven't realized that the beauty of a woman is first an inward beauty. As we own it and live out our inner beauty, we become attractive. More alluring. Our true self flows from the inside out. Although it is reflected outwardly in our appearance, it flows from a heart of love.

A woman of true beauty is at rest in her soul. She exudes a sense of calm, and a sense of rest that encourages others to be at rest. The peace of God rules her heart. Our desire should be to exhibit authentic beauty exuding from a gentle and quiet spirit, having our power under control. Godly wisdom comes as we embrace our true identity in Christ. No longer will we be fashioned by this world. We will walk completely unashamed worshipping the Lord in the beauty of holiness becoming more like our Savior every day.

"A woman of true beauty offers others the grace to be and the room to become." – Stasi Eldredge[10]

More Than a Fashion Statement

We've all heard the phrase, "clothes make the man." Do clothes really make the man or woman? Do the clothes we wear make a fashion statement? Is how we behave affected by the clothes we wear?

According to *Oxford Learner's Dictionaries*, a fashion statement is "something that you wear or own that is new or unusual and is meant to draw attention to you."[11] The objective is intended to make other people notice you.

Clothes can make a statement because they say something about us. If you learned as a teen or young adult to get attention from boys or men by the way you dressed, then you may still have that same desire as an older adult woman. It can feel good and give you a sense of power when you attract the gaze of men. But remember: the power of your sexuality and beauty was not given to you to captivate or catch the attention from men. Now some might say, didn't some Women of the Bible use their beauty for that purpose? If so, it was because God had a greater purpose in mind that would impact the lives of "others" for His glory.

Modesty is not just about clothing. Modesty, it turns out, is first and foremost an attitude of the heart that seeks to give God the glory. 1 Peter 3:3-4 says:

> "*Do not let your adorning be the outward adorning of braiding the hair, wearing gold, or putting on fine clothing. But let it be the hidden nature of the heart that which is not corruptible, even the ornament of a gentle and quiet spirit, which is very precious in the sight of God.*"

On the other side of the spectrum are women who go to an extreme to avoid looking *sexy* or *provocative*. Perhaps because of body-image issues, or a fear of unwanted attention, or a misunderstanding of what modesty means, these women don't put any effort into looking attractive. I went through this stage early in my Christian walk and ministry. But at some point, I needed to stop wearing unflattering clothing for fear of unwanted attention. It wasn't making me more holy.

As women, we certainly don't have to cross the line to feel attractive. *Kosmios*[12], the Greek word for "modesty," means "well ordered" or "of good behavior," well-arranged, seemly, or modest. It's used twice in the New Testament, both times in 1 Timothy. Similarly, in 1 Peter, the author encouraged wives to submit to their husbands so that if any of them did not believe the word of God, they could be won over by the wife's behavior. When Paul speaks of how women are to dress, it usually translates as modest.[5]

Hold up— was Paul saying that we could not get our hair braided, wear gold or pearls, or buy expensive clothing? In this case, modesty is about being appropriate and well put together. Our focus should not be on our outward appearance. Paul says, "I want women to get in there with the men in humility before God, not primping before a mirror or chasing the latest fashions but doing something beautiful for God and becoming beautiful doing it."[14]

And what does that mean? I believe certain occasions call for certain kinds of dress. For example, we might wear leggings around the house, but not to church. Unfortunately, in our culture today, between yoga pants and thongs that peek out the backside of low-rise jeans, or showing off tattoos, we've lost a little modesty when it comes to dress. When I served in full-time in-house ministry several years ago, we were very conscious of how we dressed, especially around men. That's how I learned the importance of dressing modestly. We weren't focused on our outward appearance, because our service to the Lord reflected something beautiful for God. Our clothing (along with makeup, jewelry, and so on) should be an appropriate expression of who we are without going overboard. Ask yourself a question: what do you want to communicate about yourself to the outside world? Like it or not, people form first impressions largely based on how you look. As godly women, our dress should not be the same as the world's.

We are called to be in the world, but not of the world.[15] When the word "*world*" is used in the New Testament, it's a translation of the Greek word *cosmos,* referring to planet earth and its human inhabitants. Jesus says that those who believe in Him are no longer a part of this world. The system of the world is ruled by Satan. As we read the New Testament, it is clear we are not to become entangled with the world. We may be physically present "*in the world,*" but we don't have to be a part of its value system. If we are to impact our generation for Christ, we must separate from the world's system.

Women have been influencing society with fashion since the beginning of time. Clothes are necessary. And what we wear reveals a lot about our creativity, our sense of style, our values, our body image, and our self-respect—in short, our heart. Modesty is not about a list of rules of what to wear or not wear.

You are precious in the sight of the Lord! Your beauty should not come from outward adornment. Our purity and reverence as women reveal our true identity in Christ. I know many of you may be thinking this is prudish, but true beauty radiates from the inside out.

Putting Off Deceitful Desires

> "*Put off your old self, which is being corrupted by its deceitful desires; to be made new in the attitude of your minds; and ... put on the new self, created to be like God in true righteousness and holiness.*" – Ephesians 4:22-24

We see that our "*desires can be deceitful.*" Deceitful desires can trick you, promising fulfillment they cannot deliver. We are taught to put these away as we strip off the "old self" or our former way of life when we begin to follow Jesus. No one said it would be easy. We don't instantly become free of our old ways and desires. It is a process of transformation by grace.

Understanding Your True Identity in Christ

Where are you tempted to find your identity? From your family, your friends, or society and culture? In an uncertain world, we crave the security of knowing exactly who we are and where we belong. Sadly, in today's world many women, young and old, are facing an intense struggle to find their true identity. Too often as women, we are tempted to find this safety in our roles and relationships, marriage, motherhood, professional accomplishments, beauty and fashion, body image, finding the "right" man, and so forth. The effect of these pressures can bring out feelings of worthlessness, insignificance, insecurity or unimportance, resulting in the inability to move forward. When we try to substitute these things for God and define who we are by them, we miss seeing the big picture of God's design and plan for women.

We all know from scripture that we are "*made in the image of God.*" But have you ever stopped to think about what that really means? We were created to be "*image bearers.*" As image bearers, we are created to reflect God's love, truth, and holiness into this world. As image bearers, we reflect God's character in all that we say and do. We are the "*salt of the earth*" and "*light of the world*" to those who are stumbling around in spiritual darkness.

I didn't grow up with the knowledge of my true identity in Christ until much later in life. When I was younger, I tried to find my identity in books and magazines for women, and playing sports in high school. As I grew into adulthood, I tried to find my identity in my marriage, a professional career I worked very hard to obtain the American dream. None of these things were intrinsically wrong. What was missing is that I didn't know who I was in Christ. I had no sense of God's plan or purpose for my life. I had personal dreams and desires, and professional goals that I pursued with diligence, but they didn't include God's plan and purposes for me.

At times, everyone struggles with finding their identity in what cannot ultimately satisfy. I remember as I began to grow in Christ and serve in my local church, there were times when I would make mistakes, get down on myself, and lose confidence in what I was assigned to do. My Pastor would say to me, "You don't know who you are." And you know what? He was right. I didn't know. I recall one day I was so frustrated with making mistakes and hearing this, I asked the Lord, "Who am I?" I felt so confused, like I wasn't getting it, but I kept pressing in believing that God would reveal this to me as I diligently seek Him in faith.

We discover our true identity the more we seek Him. Knowing the truth of who we really are affects the everyday reality we face as women. We have all the rights granted to us by the Father as His daughters. Eve was deceived when she did not understand who she truly was and what the Father had already provided for her.

Why is it so important for women to discover who they are created to be? For us to make a difference in a hurting world, we must first come to a place of freedom in Christ. Sadly, we are living in a day when women are severely oppressed and abused in many nations of the earth. Domestic abuse and violence, human sex trafficking of women and children, and sexual exploitation are prevalent everywhere. Unfortunately, women are still treated as second-class citizens in some cultures and religions. Our mission is to tear down every false belief and every demonic stronghold that keeps women in bondage to man-made systems. How do we do this? By putting away falsehood, and living in the truth of who Christ says we are.

Do You Realize How Valuable You Are?

Through my years in ministry serving women, I have come to recognize that the enemy deceives women into feeling powerless. Once we feel powerless, he has an open door to distort the truth of who God created us to be. I have listened to countless women struggle with poor self-esteem. They feel they have no true value in life. This seems to be a common problem among women, Christian and non-Christian, but is so far from God's truth.

This is what happens to Eve in the Garden of Eden. She allowed the serpent's words to deceive her into thinking God was holding out on them, causing her to doubt God's love. Eve's identity is thrown into confusion when she believes the lie that maybe God was keeping something away from her and Adam. Once she allows herself to doubt her value to God, the enemy deceives her into eating the fruit. Don't believe the lies of the enemy. You are valuable to God. Your worth is far above rubies.

You Are a New Creation in Christ

"Therefore, if anyone is in Christ, the new creation has come: The old has gone, the new is here!" – 2 Corinthians 5:17

We do not become new creations overnight, by doing or saying the right things. It's a process. Contrary to popular belief "all things becoming new" is not a reference to a person's lifestyle or "bad" habits changing immediately. Once a person accepts Christ as Savior, his or her lifestyle does not usually change automatically. If there needs to be change, then the only legitimate change must come from the spiritual growth based on the Word of God. I believe this passage refers to God's forgiveness of sin and giving us the opportunity to live new lives under grace.

Becoming a new creation is a matter of God's grace. Therefore, all human effort is eliminated. The reason a person becomes a new creation is that he is in union with Christ. This union means that the believer shares Christ's destiny and His inheritance. You are truly a new creation in Christ, and the old things no longer have power over you unless you allow them to. The Lord has, *"plans to prosper you and not to harm you, plans to give you hope and a future."*[16] As a child of God, remind yourself that you're not who your past failures or current circumstances say you are. You are a new creation.

We Are Kingdom Citizens

> *"Consequently, you are no longer foreigners and strangers, but fellow citizens with God's people and also members of his household." –Ephesians 2:19*

We are citizens of God's Kingdom. And as citizens, it is important to possess a Kingdom mindset. We have been reconciled to God through the cross. We are no longer foreigners and strangers, but fellow citizens with God's people and members of His household.[17]

A mindset is defined as a fixed mental attitude or disposition that predetermines or decides in advance a person's responses to and interpretations of situations.[18] Mindset is also a set of beliefs or a way of thinking that determines one's behavior, outlook, and mental attitude.

What is the Kingdom of God? The Kingdom of God is the territory governed and ruled by God, and the realm in which God's will, purposes, plans, and desires are fulfilled. Taking into consideration these definitions, we can define a Kingdom mindset as a fixed mental attitude governed by God's perspective, will, purposes, plans and desires. This mindset determines or decides a person's beliefs or way of thinking, behavior, outlook, and responses to and interpretations of situations.

We are instructed to *"seek first the Kingdom and His righteousness."* When we *"seek first"* God's way of doing and being right *"all these things will be given you as well."*[19] As Kingdom citizens, we don't have to chase things like the world because our Heavenly Father already knows what we have need of. He knows we need food, drink and clothing. I recall as a single mom never having to worry about feeding and clothing my children. I learned to trust in God to meet our needs. He never let me down. He was faithful to provide for me and my family. I trusted that He could take the little we had and multiply it in faith. I had to learn to see beyond the immediate and see God as the ultimate source for our needs.

I recall times when I had a need beyond food and clothing, like paying the bills or taking care of necessary repairs needed in our home. Once, I had to replace the air conditioning unit. I had no clue how I would pay for a new unit that cost about $4000 without going into debt and manage to buy food, clothing, and school supplies for my children. James 1:5 says, *"if you lack wisdom, you should ask God, who gives generously to all without finding fault."* Well, in seeking the Lord for wisdom, He give me specific instructions on what to do when I asked in faith. I followed those instructions, the air conditioning unit was paid for in full and we didn't miss a beat. And that's just one example. I was young and now I'm older, yet I have never seen the righteous forsaken, nor have I seen my children begging bread.[20] Nothing missing. Nothing broken. No lack.

That may not seem like much, yet when you are a single mother you struggle with knowing how you will provided for your kids. There were times in the beginning I cried out to God, "How am I going to take care of my kids?" Yet, I didn't need to worry about that, because if He feeds the birds of the air, will He not do more for His own children?

Living in the Kingdom of God is about living a life of goodness, peace, and joy in the Holy Spirit as a Kingdom citizen. We must develop a Kingdom mindset. Our thinking must be renewed to think like citizens of Heaven. It's one thing to say that Heaven is our home, and another to think, act and respond like Kingdom citizens here on earth.

Co-Laborers and Co-Heirs with Christ

We are co-laborers in Christ, carrying out His Kingdom agenda. So often, we get caught up in the world's agenda, forgetting that this world is not our home. In order to effectively co-labor with God in carrying out His Kingdom agenda, our minds must be governed by His perspective, will, purposes, plans, and desires. Now is the time to move beyond church programs and activities and become Kingdom focused!

Adoption is a wonderful way to build a family. People who choose to adopt are very special. They have a strong belief that children deserve a loving family to call their own. God created mankind because He desired to have a family. Before the fall, the Garden of Eden was a perfect place to raise a family. Yet, the fall did not catch God off-guard. It didn't take Him by surprise. God had already devised a plan to redeem mankind through His Son and adoption.

Isn't it awesome to know you have been adopted into the family of God? Romans 8:17 says, *"Now if we are children, then we are heirs—heirs of God and co-heirs with Christ, if indeed we share in his sufferings in order that we may also share in his glory."* We share in the sufferings of Christ now and will share in the glory of Christ later as heirs.

Our Father rules and reigns over the entire Kingdom of Heaven! What does it mean, then, to be co-heirs or joint-heirs with Christ? What are the promises we will inherit? The term "heirs of God" emphasizes our relationship to God the Father. As His children, we have *"an inheritance that can never perish, spoil or fade…kept in heaven."* "Heirs" in the Greek translation of Romans 8:17, refers to "those who receive their allotted possession by right of sonship." In other words, because God has made us His children, we have full rights to receive His inheritance. We are His beneficiaries.

Jesus, the only begotten Son of God, is the natural "heir" of the Father. *"God said to him, 'You are my Son; today I have become your Father.'"*[22] Hebrews 1:2 says that the Son has been *"appointed heir of all things."*

Being a co-heir with Christ means that we, as God's adopted children, will share in the inheritance of Jesus. Christ gives us His glory, His riches, and all things. We are *"accepted in the Beloved."*[23] All that belongs to Jesus Christ will belong to us, the co-heirs, as well.

"You are no longer a slave, but God's child; and since you are his child, God has made you also an heir." [24] Think of all that means. Everything that God owns belongs to us as well because we belong to Him. Our eternal inheritance as co-heirs with Christ is the result of the amazing grace of God. Ephesians 2:13 says, *"In Christ Jesus you who once were far away have been brought near by the blood of Christ."* God took us, poor orphans in this world, and made us a part of His family through faith in Jesus Christ. He has showered us with blessings and promised us an eternal inheritance, based on the worthiness of Christ Himself. Romans 8:16-17 tells us that:

> *"The Spirit himself testifies with our spirit that we are God's children. Now if we are children, then we are heirs—heirs of God and co-heirs with Christ, if indeed we share in his sufferings in order that we may also share in his glory."*

As long as you are born again, you are no longer a "slave," but a child of the Most High God. And God does not just call you His child—He also calls you "an heir" through Christ.

I started out reading the Bible to find out how to live a victorious Christian life. But now, I read it to find out more about my true identity and inheritance in Christ, and God's eternal purpose and how it relates to me. Ephesians 1:3 is a life-giving passage. The words *"every spiritual blessing"* jump off the page at me as I read it. Beloved daughters, you are an heir of the Most High God. You are a joint heir with Christ Jesus. So, find out all the blessings that your rich inheritance includes and start walking in them today.

Satan Wants to Steal Your Identity

If you've ever experienced fraudulent activity or any other form of identity theft, you know first-hand how helpless, vulnerable, and violated you're left feeling. Satan will try to hide your true identity by causing you to ask, "Did God really say…?" Satan has tried to pervert our identity since the fall in the garden.

Satan is not a creator, so he can only attempt to pervert, distort, or destroy what God has created. What Satan desires to do is take what God created for good and pervert it for evil. His purpose is to keep you from knowing who you really are in Christ. That's why it's so important that we intentionally take control of every thought, idea, or suggestion that's not in agreement with who God says we are and cast it out.

Be on the alert. Know your enemy. Satan is an adversary who is clever, crafty, deceptive and dangerous. He is a roaring lion who roams around looking for those he can devour.[25] Satan knows our weaknesses and exploits them to gain the advantage against us. The apostle Paul tells us that, "we are not unaware of his schemes."[26] When we know his tricks and schemes we can stand against the wiles of the devil.

ENDNOTES

1. *tselem Elohim*, Strong's H6754 – tselem, Blue Letter Bible , Web. July 4, 2017, https://www.blueletterbible.org/lang/lexicon/lexicon. cfm?Strongs=H6754&t=NKJV
2. Genesis 1:27
3. Hebrews 2:7
4. Luke 12::7
5. 2 Peter 1:3
6. Psalm 139:13-14
7. 1 Samuel 16:7
8. Romans 10:9-10
9. 2 Corinthians 12:9
10. Eldredge, John and Staci, *"Captivating, Unveiling the Mystery of a Woman's Soul,"* (Nashville, TN: Thomas Nelson, 2011), March 25, 2017. 137.
11. "Fashion Statement,". *Oxford Learners Dictionaries*. Oxford University Press, Web. March 25, 2017, http://www.oxfordlearnersdictionaries.com/us/definition/english/fashion-tatement?q=fashion+statement.
12. *"kosmios"*, Strongs #2887, *Bible Tools*, Web. July 5, 2017, http://www.bibletools.org/index.cfm/fuseaction/Lexicon.show/ID/G2887/kosmios.htm
13. 1 Timothy 2:9-10 MEV, The Holy Bible, Modern English Version. Copyright © 2014 by Military Bible Association. Published and distributed by Charisma House, July 5, 2017, https://www.biblegateway.com/passage/?search=1+Timothy+2%3A9-10+&version=MEV
14. 1 Timothy 2:9-10 MSG
15. John 15:19, John 17:6-19
16. Jeremiah 29:11
17. Ephesians 2:16-20
18. "Mindset," *The American Heritage Dictionary of the English Language*, Fifth Edition. (New York: Houghton Mifflin 2016), Web. July 5, 2017.
19. Matthew 6:33
20. Psalm 37:25
21. 1 Peter 1:4
22. Hebrews 5:5, Psalm 2:7
23. Ephesians 1:6
24. Galatians 4:7
25. 1 Peter 5:8
26. 2 Corinthians 2:11

Chapter 3

REVEALING THE FATHER'S HEART OF LOVE

*"For God so loved the world that he gave his one and only Son,
that whoever believes in him shall not perish but have eternal
life. For God did not send his Son into the world to condemn the
world, but to save the world through him."*
John 3:16-17

What comes to mind when you hear the word "father"? Do you immediately think of protection, provision, love, and tenderness? Or does the word "father" paint different kinds of pictures for you? One of the greatest revelations of the Bible is that God is our Father. Yet, many people have a distorted view of the heavenly Father's love because they may not have had a kind, caring earthly father. Sadly, negative childhood experiences can hold us back from our understanding of God as a Father.

God reveals Himself in the Bible as a gentle, forgiving Father, intimately involved with every detail of our lives. Unfortunately, many people do not know Him personally as Father or have a personal relationship with Him. There is a difference between knowing about God and knowing Him personally. John 1:12 says, *"Yet to all who did receive him, to those who believed in his name, he gave the right to become children of God."* We are given the right to become the children of God when we receive Him, asking Him to forgive us of our sins, and come into our hearts offering our lives as a living sacrifice to Him. We need to ask Him to forgive us of our sins and become Lord of our lives. *"If you declare with your mouth, "Jesus is Lord," and believe in your heart that God raised him from the dead, you will be saved."*[1]

We all have a need to be loved, cherished, protected, and valued. Ideally, an earthly father will meet those needs. But even if he doesn't, God will. As young children, we all long for our earthly father's approval and affection—for him to say "Son, daughter, I love you," "I'm proud of you." Yet, not everyone gets that opportunity. Some people have natural fathers who may not have been able to express their love and affection or say those words, perhaps because of the relationship they had with their father. As result, their children are left feeling empty and disappointed. They may be good men, but to them showing emotion was a sign of weakness. Unfortunately, many young men grow up with a natural understanding that a father's love is what they know from their own experience with their own father. They have grown up thinking, "Never be weak by showing emotions or tears! Be tough! Be a man!"

We need a revelation of God's love. Throughout Scripture, God describes His love for us as that of a caring parent.[2] He is our Abba Father. Imagine what your life would be like if you completely trusted God as your loving Father. The name "Abba Father" is one of the most significant names of God in understanding how He relates to his children. "Abba" is an Aramaic word that is most closely translated as "Daddy." It signifies the close, intimate relationship of a father to his child, as well as the childlike trust that a young child puts in his "daddy."

No wonder Jesus said in Matthew, "*Truly I tell you, unless you change and become like little children, you will never enter the kingdom of heaven.*" To have childlike faith, God wants us to come before Him as children, because children are innocent, and trust with a pure, uncorrupted heart.

We are His beloved children. The Holy Spirit lives in the heart of all who follow Jesus, and helps us in our weakness by interceding for us in agreement with God's will. "*The Spirit you received does not make you slaves, so that you live in fear again; rather, the Spirit you received brought about your adoption to sonship. And by him we cry, "Abba, Father.*"[3] One of the most wonderful revelations of the Bible is that God is our Father.

Even if we did not have earthly fathers who treated us well, when we have a revelation of God as Father, we have an intrinsic understanding of what a good father should be. Although King David certainly had his shortcomings as a father, he understood the paternal nature of God when he said, "*A father to the fatherless, a defender of widows, is God in his holy dwelling.*"[4]

Experiencing the Depths of God's Love

Each person's own experience with human authority is usually transferred over to how they relate to God. Good experiences bring us closer to knowing and understanding God, just as bad experiences create distorted pictures of our Father's love for us. For me, personally pursuing my relationship with our Heavenly Father has been nothing short of life-changing in every moment. It has lead me into a stronger and more passionate personal relationship with Him, and into a place of freedom with a stronger understanding of who I am. Father God wants you to be secure and confident in who you are and His love for you.

People often think they start out knowing God as Father, yet I found that I really didn't know Him as Father. I believed that He existed, but I didn't have a personal relationship with Him the way a father and daughter should have. I must admit I was a stranger. I related to Him more as God who sits on the throne in Heaven. I had very little knowledge, if any, of Him as a loving Father. We can know a great deal about God through reading the Bible or reading books about Him without true knowledge of Him.

As I pursued Him, I came to know Him by experience through heartbreaks, disappointments, joy and pain. Now I know Him intimately as a loving Father who cares for His children. I came to know and rely on the love God has for me. What a privilege to call Him Father!

What an awesome demonstration of love! While we were still sinners, God revealed His great love for us.[5] Everyone has a need to be loved. Two of our greatest needs are to know who we are and that we are loved. Before beginning this journey, I had no knowledge of who I was in Christ, nor how much I was loved by Him. I didn't have the power to "*to grasp how wide and long and high and deep*" the love of Christ is.[6] I wanted to know more about God so I read J.I. Packer's classic *Knowing God*. What I learned about God's love, grace, goodness, wisdom and wrath drew me closer to Him, giving me the courage to pursue more of Him daily. The material in this book stretched my understanding and changed my life. We were created to know God intimately and should set our hearts to knowing and pursuing Him.

I recall a time I was so hurt by an experience in which I felt unloved by the very person who had made a commitment to love me for better or worse. I was so wounded. As I sat on my bathroom floor one day, the love of Christ reached down and the Father said to me, "*No one will ever love you the way that I love you.*" I sensed His presence all around me that day enabling me to come out of the depths of despair.

I committed to moving forward with my life, no matter what the outcome would bring. The love God was referring to is *agape* love; the highest form of God's love for man. Agape love does not refer to romantic or sexual love. Nor does it refer to close friendship or brotherly love. Agape love involves faithfulness, commitment, and an act of the will as described in 1 Corinthians 1:13.

God Passionately Loves You

The Bible is full of scriptures that reveal God's love for us. His love is everlasting. I would like to share a few to encourage you in how much you are loved by God:

> *"See what great love the Father has lavished on us, that we should be called children of God! And that is what we are!" – I John 3:1a*

> *"This is love: not that we loved God, but that he loved us and sent his Son as an atoning sacrifice for our sins. Dear friends, since God so loved us, we also ought to love one another. No one has ever seen God; but if we love one another, God lives in us, and his love is made complete in us." – 1 John 4:10-12*

> *"For I am convinced that neither death nor life, neither angels nor demons, neither the present nor the future, nor any powers, neither height nor depth, nor anything else in all creation, will be able to separate us from the love of God that is in Christ Jesus our Lord." Romans 8:38-39*

> *"For great is his love toward us, and the faithfulness of the LORD endures forever." – Psalm 117:2*

Ephesians 3:17-19 also encourages every believer to be *"rooted and grounded"* in love and be able to comprehend *"what is the width and length and depth and height—to know the love of Christ."*

The Greatest Commandment is Love
—Loving Others as God Loves Us

"Love knows no limits to its endurance, no end to its trust, no fading of its hope; it can outlast anything. It is, in fact, the one thing that stands when all else has fallen." Elisabeth Elliot[7]

Our world has a distorted meaning of love but God's Word remains a true and steadfast source of knowledge in how to love. In a time of controversy and uncertainty, one thing remains constant: *"God is love,"* and we are commanded to love one another as we love ourselves. Jesus being fully God and fully man is the embodiment of love. The Bible not only says that God loves, but that God is love, which makes Him the perfect source for us to learn how to love others, even those who are difficult for us to love. *"Dear friends, let us love one another, for love comes from God. Everyone who loves has been born of God and knows God. Whoever does not love does not know God, because God is love."*[8] Jesus is very clear in Scripture that we are to love God and love one another as we love ourselves.

Jesus fed the hungry and healed the sick on the Sabbath.[9] It may be hard for us to understand this today, but at the time, these were serious offenses. The Pharisees accused Jesus of breaking the law by healing on the Sabbath. Jesus had a different view, however. He was fulfilling the Law rather than contradicting it. He was fulfilling the commandment to love others by showing goodwill and benevolence to those less fortunate. Perhaps feeding the hungry and healing the sick is what made the day Holy, after all?

I was saddened by the onslaught of rhetoric, hateful words, and verbal attacks even by Christians via social media during and following the 2016 elections. We need to be reminded of what the Bible says in Galatians 5:13-15:

"You, my brothers and sisters, were called to be free. But do not use your freedom to indulge the flesh; rather, serve one another humbly in love. For the entire law is fulfilled in keeping this one command: 'Love your neighbor as yourself.' If you bite and devour each other, watch out or you will be destroyed by each other."

Jesus is calling believers to be immersed in love, evidenced not only by our words, but also by our actions. *"God anointed Jesus of Nazareth with the Holy Spirit and power, and…he went around doing good and healing all who were under the power of the devil, because God was with him."*[10]

God's Undying Love

God's greatest desire was to reconcile His people back to Himself. The story of Hosea and Gomer epitomizes God's undying love for His children. God used the prophet Hosea to illustrate His love and desire to have His people restored.

When God first speaks to Hosea in Hosea 1:2, He tells him to *"Go, marry a promiscuous woman and have children with her, for like an adulterous wife this land is guilty of unfaithfulness to the Lord."* I don't know how many of us would be thrilled to be given an assignment like this, but Hosea is commanded to marry a woman whom God tells him will be unfaithful. I'm sure as a godly man and prophet, Hosea has different hopes for marriage, perhaps pursuing a wife who will share not only his heart but also his faith and convictions. Aware of Gomer's promiscuous reputation and scandalous behavior, Hosea humbles himself in obedience to the Lord. Hosea does exactly as God commanded. He marries Gomer, and eventually, three children are born. After the third child is born, Hosea and Gomer's marriage falls apart. No doubt, Hosea is heartbroken. He never forgets her and never stops loving her.

God's purpose for Hosea's marriage to Gomer was to confront Israel with their sin of unfaithfulness. This may sound like a familiar story for some of you. With regards to marriage, this is a special case, with a special purpose. God didn't call everyone to do what He assigned Hosea to do.

Later, in Hosea 3:1, God tells Hosea to find Gomer and buy her back after she had left him to return to her old way of life, *"Go, show your love to your wife again, though she is loved by another man and is an adulteress. Love her as the Lord loves the Israelites, though they turn to other gods and love the sacred raisin cakes."* Hosea reconciles with Gomer and instructs her that she is not to commit adultery again, but that she will live with him and he will live with her for many days. God reveals to Hosea that the time is right, so he redeems Gomer out of slavery.

Hosea's message to the children of Israel was linked very closely with His personal life. Hosea married a woman who he knew would eventually betray his trust. They would have three children that would be given names that sent messages of judgment on Israel. Though God would bring judgment on sin, He will always bring His people back to Himself. What does this reveal? God's undying love, grace and faithfulness to His children. Israel, God's chosen people, had been unfaithful to Him through idolatry. In the same way Hosea was instructed to redeem his estranged wife and sought to continue his relationship with her, God promised to redeem Israel and renew their relationship with Him. The story of Hosea and Gomer is a powerful picture of God's endless love for His covenant people. Our God is a jealous God! We are in covenant relationship with Him and faithfulness is important.

God Loves Broken People

When the world that I had known fell apart, it didn't feel good, but the broken pieces needed to be picked up. Thank God, He was there to help me pick up the shattered pieces. I will never forget that moment when He said to me, *"No one will ever love you the way that I love you."* There is no doubt in my heart the Father loves me. The song I sang as a child, "Jesus loves me, this I know" is more real to me than when I was a child. I know this not just because the Bible tells me, but from experience. I know I am loved. Just as much as God loves Jesus, He loves you with an undying passion. Jesus was "*sent to bind up the brokenhearted, to proclaim freedom for the captives and release from darkness for the prisoners.*"[11]

It's difficult to continue to love someone who doesn't love us back in the same way. In our natural state, we can't do this, but in the Spirit of Christ, this is possible based on 1 Corinthians 13. We cannot escape the message of God's undying love in Hosea 3. Gomer is still loved by Hosea, even though she is an adulteress. God wants him to seek her out and prove his love to her time and time again. How can anyone love that deeply? The answer is right there in God's instructions to Hosea, "*even as the Lord loves.*" When you have known the love and forgiveness of God by experience; it empowers you to love this completely. When you've experienced His loving forgiveness, you cannot help but love and forgive others. Hosea is an outstanding biblical example of that kind of love.

God's response to you and I is the same as it was to Israel. He will heal your unfaithfulness. He will love you freely. He values you so much that He enters into covenant with you, redeems you, and remains faithful to you.

> "*There is no fear in love. But perfect love drives out fear, because fear has to do with punishment. The one who fears is not made perfect in love.*" – 1 John 4:18

We all have struggled with some form of fear or insecurity, whether it be fear that God won't come through for you or fear of lack. At times, I was anxious about my past, my future, my finances, or what people thought about me. The good news is that we do not have to fear that God doesn't love us or that He won't come through for us in our time of need. God's perfect love drives out fear.

God's presence in our lives is diminished when we operate out of fear. Satan uses fear to attack us, but God *"has not given us a spirit of fear."*[12] His Spirit gives us *"power, love and a sound mind."* Satan works overtime trying to convince us that God doesn't love us, but we have not been given the spirit of bondage to fear. Confess with your mouth the truth that God does love you during these attacks of fear.

Knowing God as Father

What can we actually know about someone? Imagine strolling through the mall and running into someone you should know, but can't remember their name. Think of a time when someone you had met only once before greeted you the next time by name, but you couldn't remember theirs. I've had that happen a few times. It can be an embarrassing moment.

Knowing someone by name indicates a personal relationship with that person. People tend to feel more valued and respected when someone remembers their name. The trouble is, most of us have difficulty remembering the names of people we don't know well. Sometimes we may even avoid someone whose name we don't remember simply to avoid embarrassment. We even make excuses like, "I'm terrible at names." Or "I have a bad memory."

What about the names of God? Each name of God reveals a defining quality of His nature and character, as we can see throughout the Old Testament. He shows us who He is and gives us an understanding of His character by giving Himself specific and descriptive names such as:

Elohim – God and Mighty Creator
El Shaddai – God Almighty
El Roi – the God Who Sees Me
Yahweh Rophe – the Lord Who Heals
Yahweh Shalom – the Lord Is Peace.
Yeshua Hamashiach – Jesus the Messiah[13]

Jesus came into the world to offer salvation and deliverance to anyone who calls upon His name. He is the Son of God. The Messiah, the Christ, the Anointed One! He is loved by our Heavenly Father, precious and honored in His sight. The Father gives people and nations for His life. *"Since you are precious and honored in my sight, and because I love you, I will give people in exchange for you, nations in exchange for your life."*[14] He will bring His sons and daughters from the ends of the earth. Jesus came to proclaim good news to the poor in spirit, freedom to those who are bound, recovery of sight to those who are blind, and to set the captives free.[15]

Why I Call God "Father"

In Scripture, there are many different names used to describe God. While all the names of God are important in many ways, the name "Abba Father" is one of the most significant names of God in understanding how He relates to people. The word *Abba* is an Aramaic word that would most closely be translated as "Daddy." It was a common term used by young children to address their fathers. It signifies the close, intimate relationship of a father to his child, as well as the childlike trust that a young child puts in his "daddy."[16]

What a powerful name it is—the name of Jesus Christ. Jesus came into the world to offer salvation and deliverance to anyone who believes and calls upon His name. Just speaking the name Jesus shifts the atmosphere. It silences the voice of doubt and unbelief, and the fiery darts of the enemy causing faith to arise.

Being a child of God is the highest privilege and honor that can be imagined. We have been, adopted through faith in Christ Jesus which is the source of our hope, the security of our future and the motivation to walk worthy of your calling.[17] Being a daughter of the King of Kings and Lord of Lords calls us to a higher standard, a different way of life, and a greater hope in His unfailing love. It is amazing that a holy and righteous God who is all-powerful, all-knowing, and ever-present, would allow us sinful humans the privilege to call Him "Daddy." "*I will be a Father to you, and you will be my sons and daughters, says the Lord Almighty.*"[18] He is our "Abba Father," and He is the Perfect Father! That's why I call Him Father.

God is Faithful

We know a characteristic of God is faithfulness. The Israelites were promised a land flowing with milk and honey if they lived by faith and move ahead to possess the land God had promised them. In some ways, my journey has been similar to the children of Israel coming out of Egypt. Egypt represented a place of oppression and slavery for the children of Israel. Because of the Lord's love and faithfulness, He bought them out with a mighty hand.

> "*But it was because the Lord loved you and kept the oath he swore to your ancestors that he brought you out with a mighty hand and redeemed you from the land of slavery, from the power of Pharaoh king of Egypt. Know therefore that the Lord your God is God; he is the faithful God, keeping his covenant of love to a thousand generations of those who love him and keep his commandments.*"[19]

The Israelites had to overcome the giants in the land to continue their journey to their Promise Land. The giants struck fear in the hearts of the Israelites, causing some of them to draw back. On our journey, we may experience discouragement, fear, impatience, and unbelief, just as the children of Israel did, as we walk in faith and encounter our own giants.

I still face obstacles as I pursue what God has called me to. But I am determined to move ahead despite the obstacles.

" Therefore, since we are surrounded by such a great cloud of witnesses, let us throw off everything that hinders and the sin that so easily entangles. And let us run with perseverance the race marked out for us, fixing our eyes on Jesus, the pioneer and perfector of faith. For the joy set before him, He endured the cross, scorning its shame, and sat down at the right hand of the throne of God." [20]

God has set a race before each of His children. Run with endurance—relentless perseverance—to finish your race well. God knows the plans He has for you, and He is faithful to bring them to pass as you stay the course He set for you.

"I alone know the plans I have for you, plans to bring you prosperity and not disaster, plans to bring about the future you hope for. Then you will call to me. You will come and pray to me, and I will answer you. You will seek me, and you will find me because you will seek me with all your heart." [21]

During this journey, you may be tempted to give up, quit, or stray from the path God has ordained, but remember there is no temptation that can keep you from your God-given destiny. When you are tempted, God will provide a way for you to endure or escape the temptation, if you hold on. God is faithful; He will not let you be tempted beyond what you can bear. When you are tempted, look for His provision of a way out.

The Bible is full of examples of God's faithfulness to His children. Psalm 119:90 says His *"faithfulness continues through all generations."* My favorite verse regarding God's faithfulness, one that I always lean into as I travel this journey, is found in Joshua 1. Joshua is chosen to lead the children of Israel into the Promised Land after the death of Moses. The Lord says to Joshua, *"Have I not commanded you? Be strong and courageous. Do not be afraid; do not be discouraged, for the Lord your God will be with you wherever you go."* [22]

God Is Unchanging

> *"Jesus Christ is the same yesterday and today and forever."*
> *– Hebrews 13:8*

God is immutable. It is impossible for His character, will and covenant promises to change. He is immutably wise, merciful, good and gracious. His power cannot be augmented or diminished. He never forgets, and He cannot be anything other than perfectly holy. Human beings can change in a multitude of ways, but our Father remains ever the same.

Numbers 13:19 says, *"God is not human, that he should lie, not a human being, that he should change his mind. Does he speak and then not act? Does he promise and not fulfill?"*

Hebrews 6:17-18 says, *"Because God wanted to make the unchanging nature of his purpose very clear to the heirs of what was promised, he confirmed it with an oath. God did this so that, by two unchangeable things in which it is impossible for God to lie, we who have fled to take hold of the hope set before us may be greatly encouraged."*

It is His unchanging love that leads Him to call out His people from their sin and bondage.[23] God Himself tells us that He does not change. *"I the LORD do not change."*[24] He will always do what He says He will do. If He spoke it, He will do it.

You Are a Child of God

> *"God loves each of us as if there was only one of us."*
> *– Saint Augustine*[25]

In today's culture, many young girls and women grow up with negative beliefs about themselves that carry over into adulthood. They are vulnerable to defining themselves in comparison to others. They vie for attention by acting and dressing inappropriately. The effects of social media, reality television, and celebrity culture tend to reinforce these methods. They try to be "good enough" in a world that says, "You're not good enough." They long for unconditional love, acceptance, and inclusion, which shapes the way they define themselves, their attractiveness to others, and what they feel they are capable of doing and becoming.

Sadly, we live in a world that's full of *"you're not"* messages. You're not valuable. You're not attractive or pretty. You're not smart enough for this job. You're not competent enough to be a leader. And the list goes on. Today, God is saying *"You're everything I've created to you be!"*

The Book to the Ephesians is filled with precious jewels that encourages us to know our identity in Christ. Ephesians 1:6 says, *"he hath made us accepted in the beloved"* to the praise and glory of His grace. The word that stands out to me is, *"accepted."*

Too many of us spend our entire lives trying to earn acceptance from others like our parents, peers, life partners, co-workers, and people we respect. Sadly, many of us struggle with trusting the truth that we're acceptable to and accepted by God, perhaps because of our past. The truth is, you are God's beloved not because of what you do or how you look. It's because God the Father says so. When you truly embrace your identity in Christ, you realize acceptance is what you already have and you don't have to earn it. *"If God says his chosen ones are acceptable to him, can anyone bring charges against them? Or can anyone condemn them? No indeed!"*[26]

When you accepted Christ, God accepted you. You may sometimes feel rejected, but how you feel is not who you are. God doesn't show favoritism. We are all accepted in the beloved, and He shows no partiality, *"but accepts from every nation the one who fears him and does what is right."*[27]

I am the mother of two sons with vastly differently personalities, yet I love them both distinctively and uniquely. To love them equally, or the same, implies that they are indistinguishable. That's not true. Just as we love our children who are different from one another, God loves each one of His children uniquely. Each one of us has personal value to Him. I have been blessed, humbled, and fortunate to come to a place of understanding which gives me a strong sense of security and value, and a sense of destiny and purpose. God loves us with an everlasting love.

No Longer an Orphan

Adoption is a great way to build a family. There are many children in America and other countries that are waiting to be adopted by a loving family. The process of adoption can take a long time, and can cause stress and strain on the adoptive family. Often, when parents adopt a child, they go through a selection process before adopting a child to decide which child they would like to adopt. The wonderful thing about being adopted into God's family is that God decided in advance to adopt us through Jesus Christ.

Father God wants His sons and daughters to understand who they are. He wants us to know our true identity. Jesus is the perfect example of a son knowing his true identity and position in the Kingdom of God. The Bible says, *"to as many as receive Him, He gives the power to be sons and daughters of God."*[28]

Many of us have experienced rejection at one point in time or another. It's a powerful weapon against our self-worth and can breed thoughts of inadequacy, hopelessness, anger, bitterness, fear, and depression. No matter where it comes from, rejection can cause great damage in how we see ourselves and our value to others.

Each time we experience rejection, the potential for doubt and unbelief increases. How can you have faith in life, others, or yourself when you believe you are unlovely, incapable, or inadequate in some way? The seeds of rejection produce the harvest of failure. This is nothing more than bondage and oppression. We often carry this same attitude into our relationship with God. Jesus said, "*I will not leave you as orphans; I will come to you.*"[29]

We are not orphans. We were predestined for adoption. Here are some passages that highlight our heavenly adoption:

> "*For he chose us in him before the creation of the world to be holy and blameless in his sight. In love, he predestined us for adoption to sonship through Jesus Christ, in accordance with his pleasure and will— to the praise of his glorious grace, which he has freely given us in the One he loves.*" – Ephesians 1:4-6

> "*But when the set time had fully come, God sent his Son, born of a woman, born under the law, to redeem those under the law, that we might receive adoption to sonship. Because you are his sons, God sent the Spirit of his Son into our hearts, the Spirit who calls out, 'Abba, Father.' So you are no longer a slave, but God's child; and since you are his child, God has made you also an heir.*" – Galatians 4:4-8

> "*For those who are led by the Spirit of God are the children of God. The Spirit you received does not make you slaves, so that you live in fear again; rather, the Spirit you received brought about your adoption to sonship. And by him we cry, "Abba, Father." The Spirit himself testifies with our spirit that we are God's children. Now if we are children, then we are heirs— heirs of God and co-heirs with Christ, if indeed we share in his sufferings in order that we may also share in his glory.*" – Romans 8:14-17

To redeem means to obtain or to set free by paying a price. What was the price that God paid for our freedom and adoption? – the price of his Son's life.

You Are a Daughter Becoming a Son

One day, the Lord said to me, *"You are a daughter becoming a son."* I thought to myself, what an odd statement? I didn't understand what it meant to be a *"daughter becoming a son."* I know that I am His daughter, but knowing and understanding sonship was something I didn't quite grasp.

> *"Now that faith has come, we are no longer under the control of a tutor or guardian...for we are born-again or spiritually transformed, renewed, set apart for His purpose with full rights and privileges through faith in Jesus Christ...we have taken on His characteristics and values...we are all one in Christ (we who believe) ...we are Abraham's seed and spiritual heirs according to God's promise."* [30]

We are no longer under the law. We have been redeemed and liberated with all rights as fully grown members of God's family. Abba's desire is that we fully understand who we are in Him. He is calling His people to know their identity in order for them to step into their God-given destiny as sons and daughters.

> *The world "waits in eager expectation for the children of God to be revealed. For the creation was subjected to frustration, not by its own choice, but by the will of the one who subjected it, in hope that the creation itself will be liberated from its bondage to decay and brought into the freedom and glory of the children of God."* [31]

God is inviting all born-again children of God to walk in sonship. To walk in sonship requires maturity.

> *"In bringing many sons and daughters to glory, it was fitting that God, for whom and through whom everything exists, should*

make the pioneer of their salvation perfect through what he suffered. Both the one who makes people holy and those who are made holy are of the same family. So Jesus is not ashamed to call them brothers and sisters." [32]

It was fitting for Christ to suffer so that we might become sons and daughters of God. He is the captain of our salvation. Maturing as sons and daughters is important to fulfilling your God-given destiny.

God has kept us and is ready to release all the blessings and promises He has ordained for His children. The revelation that this is our right because we are His sons in Christ should shake and wake us up out of any place of dullness in our walk with Him. The glory of the inheritance that is ours was pre-determined before He even formed the world.

Romans 8 declares that the suffering we experience is not to be compared to the incredible glory God intends to reveal in His sons and daughters, those who walk in mature sonship. This nameless, faceless generation of holy people will move in the Spirit's power yet seek no glory for themselves.

We need the mindset of a son to possess our birthright. Our culture generally causes us to think like slaves, not sons. I am reminded that I can never earn my identity as a son, it is simply offered through the redemption of Jesus offered by a loving father. I urge you, walk in this freedom. Don't believe the lie that you must earn God's love and approval. Do not walk in a spirit of slavery and fear, but walk as a son—a son of a Good Father.

God's Nature Is to Bless

1 John 3:1 says, *"See what great love the Father has lavished on us, that we should be called children of God!"* To lavish means to give generously and in abundance. It's God's nature to bless His children. He wants to

richly bless us with His Kingdom. That has always been God's original intention. Genesis 1:28 says, "*God blessed them*" after creating mankind. A blessing is "the act or words of one that blesses," or "a thing conducive to happiness or welfare."[33]

As a child of God, you are adopted into His family and have inherited every spiritual blessing in Christ. He has endowed you with benefits that can never be taken away from you. Paul says in Ephesians 1:3, that Father God has, "*blessed us in the heavenly realms with every spiritual blessing in Christ.*" The Greek word for "blessing" is the word *eulogia* [34] which means "to speak well of, benefit." God has spoken good things about us and for our benefit.

Sadly, many in the church have settled for a life less than what Christ purchased with His blood. We must remember there are countless blessings that belong us and live like it. As a daughter of the King, you are the recipient of every spiritual blessing in Christ.

It's the Father's Heart to Bless His Children

It's the Father's heart to bless His children abundantly, beyond measure. Sometimes we can become so enamored with the physical blessings of prosperity that we forget about the spiritual blessings we have in Christ. In the Book of Job, Satan desired to prove that Job only served God because of His blessings. God gave Satan permission to test Job to prove him wrong. Job's friends were certain that Job must have sinned, as that was the only reason they could think of for God to remove His blessings. They were wrong. In all of this, Job did not sin or curse God. In the end, the "*Lord blessed the latter part of Job's life more than the former part.*"[35]

King David knew all too well the importance of not forgetting God's benefits. When I think of the goodness of Jesus and all He's done for me, my soul cries *Hallelujah!* Thank God for saving me. We are to pass on the blessing of these benefits to the next generation, leaving a rich spiritual inheritance for our children and children's children. This inheritance can be a legacy of faith.

When I look back over my own life, I see how my grandmother left a legacy of faith in God for me and my children. Living with my grandmother as a young girl. She would watch the Billy Graham Crusade faithfully whenever it came on TV. She made sure my brothers, sisters, and I went to Vacation Bible School in the summer and attended church services on Sunday with her at our local church, as well as Homecoming service and revival services in the fall. Seeds of faith were sown that I couldn't even begin to comprehend at the time.

ENDNOTES

1. Romans 10:9
2. John 16:26-27, 2 Corinthians 6:18
3. Romans 8:15
4. Psalm 68:5
5. Romans 5:6-8
6. Ephesians 3:18
7. Elliott, Elizabeth, *Let Me Be a Woman*, *Goodreads*, Web. March 25, 2017, www.goodreads.com/quotes/277266-this-love-of-which-i-speak-is-slow-to-lose.
8. 1 John 4:7-8
9. Matthew 12:1-13
10. Acts 10:38
11. Isaiah 61:1
12. 2 Timothy 1:7
13. "If His name was Yeshua, why do we call Him Jesus?", *Got Questions*, Web. July 9, 2017, www.gotquestions.org/Yeshua-Jesus.html.
14. Isaiah 43:4
15. Luke 4:18
16. "*What does it mean that God is our Abba Father?*", Got Questions, Web. July 8, 2017. www.gotquestions.org/Abba-Father.html.
17. Ephesians 4:1
18. 2 Corinthians 6:18
19. Deuteronomy 7:8-9
20. Hebrews 12:1-2
21. Jeremiah 29:11-13
22. Joshua 1:9
23. "God Unchanging" *Ligonier Ministries the teaching fellowship of R.C. Sproul*, Web. July 8, 2017, www.ligonier.org/learn/devotionals/god-unchanging/.
24. Malachi 3:6
25. Augustine, St. *BrainyQuotes*, Web. March 25, 2017, www.brainyquote.com/quotes/quotes/s/saintaugus105351.html.
26. Romans 8:33-34 CEV
27. Acts 10:35
28. John 1:12
29. John 3:18 AMP

30. Galatians 3:23-29 AMP

31. Romans 8:19-21

32. Hebrews 2:10-11

33. "Blessing," *Merriam-Webster.com*, Merriam-Webster Dictionary, Web. March 25, 2017.

34. 2129. *eulogia*, Strong Concordance, *Bible Hub*, Web. July 9, 2017, http://biblehub.com/greek/2129.html.

35. Job 42:12

Chapter 4

GOD'S TRANSFORMING LOVE

"Forgiveness is an act of the will, and the will can function regardless of the temperature of the heart."
Corrie Ten Boom[1]

The Bible says, *"all have sinned and fall short of the glory of God."*[2] Forgiveness is the act of pardoning an offender. The Greek word translated "forgiveness" literally means "to let go," as when a person does not demand payment for a debt.[3] The Lord our God is merciful and forgiving and we should strive to be the same.

God's love is irresistible. His love brings about transformation in our lives. The love of Christ gives us the foundation for believing God has forgiven us. Sometimes we believe we've failed God so badly that He'll never forgive us. However, God tells us over and over that His mercy is much bigger than our worst mistakes. He alone does great wonders. He remembered us

77

in our lowly state. His love and mercy is enduring!

Always Forgiving

God doesn't want anyone to sin, but He knows we will. That's why He provided a way for us to have complete forgiveness through His Son, Jesus. And He not only gives us a way out, He's excited about forgiving us. Who is like the Lord? He delights in showing us mercy.

> *"Who is a God like you, who pardons sin and forgives the transgression of the remnant of his inheritance? You do not stay angry forever, but delight to show mercy. You will again have compassion on us; you will tread our sins underfoot and hurl all our iniquities into the depths of the sea."* [4]

When I read these verses, I get a mental picture of God stomping on my sins and throwing them into the sea, where they'll never be seen again. What a great God!

Forgiveness is one of the most powerful responses that we could ever have as believers. Forgiving others is never easy, but it's not impossible. We forgive others when we let go of resentment and give up any claim to be compensated for the hurt or loss we have suffered. Forgiving shows that the love, grace, and mercy of Jesus are operating in our lives.

God gives you divine power to forgive and set free those who have deeply wounded you. The love of Christ working through you is the power that truly sets the captive free and can affect the whole world. Forgiveness defeats darkness on a massive scale because it involves the resurrection power of Jesus. Nothing can defeat the greatness and glory there is in one act of forgiveness.

When God forgives you, it empowers you to forgive others. Forgiveness transforms anger and hurt into healing and peace. Forgiveness can help you overcome feelings of depression, anxiety, and rage, as well as personal and relational conflicts. Forgiveness is about making the conscious decision to let go of a grudge. It may be that your resentment is justified. The person may have done a very evil, terrible thing to you. You may have every legal and intellectual right to hold a grudge and to hate that person. But if you want to see miracles in your life, it is necessary that you forgive. Matthew 6:14-15 says, "*For if you forgive other people when they sin against you, your heavenly Father will also forgive you. But if you do not forgive others their sins, your Father will not forgive your sins.*"

Forgiveness is a process that cleanses you. It doesn't make the other person right. It doesn't mean you are excusing and approving the wrong behavior of another person. Nor is it saying that the offense is not important. Forgiveness sets you free in your heart to move forward with grace. God wijll give you the grace to fully set others free.

When someone has offended you, be honest with yourself and make sure not to allow a root of bitterness spring up and cause trouble for you.[5] Talk with God honestly when you feel offended, and let Him heal and restore you to a place of love, peace and wholeness. Forgiveness triggers God's healing power to help you release an offense and not sink deeper into a pit of despair by harboring the offense in your heart.[6]

Forgiveness Changes Everything

Most of us accept Jesus' resurrection, but have we fully grasped and embraced its power and impact? The resurrection of Jesus Christ was one of the most momentous events in history. Jesus fulfilled a vital part of God's plan when He rose from the dead. God has a redemptive plan for mankind. God's plan of redemption included both Jesus' birth, death and resurrection. In the Bible, the word translated as "resurrection" comes from the Greek word "*anastasis,*" which means "raising up" or "standing up again."[7]

Jesus taught His disciples about His coming resurrection, but for a while they failed to really understand even though they had been with Him for three years. Keep in mind, they had not received the promise of the Holy Spirit at that time. The resurrection of Jesus was at the heart of Paul's teachings. Paul said, *"I want to know Christ—yes, to know the power of his resurrection and participation in his sufferings, becoming like him in his death."*[8]

In Ephesians 1, Paul prays that God would impart a deeper knowledge and understanding of Christ. That should be our prayer, too. To know Him intimately so that you can see exactly what it is He is calling you to do, and to grasp the vastness of this glorious way of life He has promised His followers.

Unforgiveness

Offense is the bait of Satan. Satan sets up traps or hindrances in our lives to bring offense. The word *"offend"* is the Greek word *"skandalon"* which means *"a stick for bait (of a trap), a snare, a stumbling block, an offense, a means of entrapment."*[9] Luke 17:1 says, *"Things that cause people to stumble are bound to come."*

The occasions for taking offense are endless. We are daily given the opportunity to be offended by something or someone, whether in the line at the grocery store, driving on the freeway, at work, or even in church. The traps of offense are often small things that can weigh us down if not dealt with properly.

Maybe someone fails to meet our expectations, or we don't like the personality of someone. We may get hurt by something someone says that offends us. Taking offense against another person can turn into unforgiveness and bitterness. Many are wounded, hurt, or bitter, not knowing they have fallen into a trap.

During my early years in ministry, there were many opportunities for me to become offended by the slights by others I felt until I read John Bevere's book, *"The Bait of Satan."* This book truly opened my understanding of how Satan uses offense through close relationships. Living among over one hundred people is a prime opportunity to take offense. David lamented in Psalm 55:12-14 saying, *"If an enemy were insulting me, I could endure it; if a foe were rising against me, I could hide. But it is you, a man like myself, my companion, my close friend, with whom I once enjoyed sweet fellowship at the house of God, as we walked about among the worshipers."* In his book, John Bevere says, "The closer the relationship, the more severe the offense!"[10] This was an eye opener for me.

Often, we like to pretend that we don't get offended. In Matthew 16:23, even Jesus became offended. Jesus had just revealed to His disciples that *"He must go to Jerusalem and suffer many things at the hands of the elders, the chief priests, and the teachers of the law, and that He must be killed and on the third day raised to life."*[11] Contrary to the disciples' expectations, Peter took Jesus aside and began to rebuke Him. Jesus turned to Peter and said, *"Get behind me, Satan! You are a stumbling (offense) block to me."* Unwittingly, Peter did not understand this was God's plan and was acting as an agent for Satan.

Satan is cunning. At times, he uses women against one another as a snare to offend by encouraging women to judge each other, make curt (rudely brief) remarks towards each other, or quarrel with each other over foolish things. When this happens, we unknowingly become captive to the devil to do his will. 2 Timothy 2:26 says, *"they will come to their senses and escape from the trap of the devil, who has taken them captive to do his will."*

One way Satan keeps a person in a state of offense is to hide or cloak the offense with pride, keeping them from admitting you are offended. Pride keeps you from dealing with the truth, causing you to feel like a victim and justify your behavior. We tell ourselves, "I'm fine. I'm not hurt." All the while, we are seething on the inside.

The Lord began to deal with me by showing me that I had to see my true condition. If we are going to do battle with the enemy in the army of the Lord, then we will need to learn to deal with offense as it comes. Because it will come! Jesus said to his disciples, "*things that cause people to stumble are bound to come, but woe to anyone through whom they come.*"[12]

Why Do We Find It So Hard to Forgive?

One reason we resist forgiving is that we don't really understand what forgiveness is or how it works. We think we do, but we don't. If you're like many people, you may want to be free of past offenses, but you still carry bitter memories or hard feelings toward those who have wronged you. Take comfort: forgiving even the worst offenses against you is not impossible. It is possible to find freedom from the past and peace that comes from God by learning to really forgive from the heart.

Consider my experience. Years ago, my ex-husband had an affair that resulted in the birth of a child. We tried to make it work, but the damage was already done. I found it difficult to forgive since bitterness took root in my heart. One day, I flipped out, and it was then I knew it was time to get control of what was happening in my heart.

It takes heroic effort to move beyond our own pain to understand what prevents us from saying "I forgive you." It didn't happen overnight, but I was able to eventually forgive and embrace the child. I believe in my heart it was important for the sake of my children. I can see now, if I had chosen the path of bitterness, it would have not only defiled me, but also my children and their sister. I am thankful because now we all have a loving relationship with one another.

Hebrews 12:14-15 says, "*Make every effort to live in peace with all men and to be holy; without holiness, no one will see the Lord. See to it that no one misses the grace of God and that no bitter root grows up to cause trouble and defile many.*" The awe-inspiring thing is that through God's help and through our relationship with Jesus, we can overcome bitterness by applying God's Word to our circumstances.

My dear sisters, I urge you by the mercies of God, never let bitterness take root in your heart. God has a bigger plan for your life. Don't let bitterness spoil what God has purposed for you! "*I will say of the LORD, "He is my refuge and my fortress, my God, in whom I trust." Surely he will save you from the fowler's snare and from the deadly pestilence.*"[13]

The Power of Repentance

After John the Baptist was put in prison, Jesus came to Galilee, preaching the gospel of the Kingdom of God saying, "*The time has come... the kingdom of God has come near. Repent, and believe in the good news.*" [14] In fact, John the Baptist centered much of his preaching on repentance. To repent means to change directions completely. It involves a dramatic and decisive change of course. God urges us to repent when the path we are taking leads to destruction. John Henry Thayer, an American Biblical scholar commented on repentance as:

> "*...the change of mind of those who have begun to abhor their errors and misdeeds, and have determined to enter upon a better course of life, so that it embraces both a recognition of sin and sorrow for it and hearty amendment, the tokens and effects of which are good deeds (1958, 406).*"[15]

There is divine power in repentance. The atonement and sacrifice of Jesus made it possible for people to receive salvation. The Lord suffered and endured the cross, despising the shame so that we might be set free through repentance. When we acknowledge our sins, turn to God in humility and heartfelt repentance the blood of Jesus cleanses us from sin through the power of forgiveness.

Paul wrote that, "*godly sorrow brings repentance.*"[16] The problem is that we think of repentance as something negative. Repentance involves a radical change of heart and mind in which we agree with God's assessment of our sin and then take specific action to align ourselves with His truth. Just having a desire to change is not repentance. Repentance is always an active response to God's Word. The evidence of repentance is not words of resolve, but a changed life.

Repentance Is Not a Dirty Word

What do you think when you think of the word "repent?" Does it suggest a picture of an angry God fed up with your sinful ways, ready to condemn you to hell if you don't repent? The very word can evoke a response of fear in many when they sin, rather than knowing that repentance is an opportunity to turn around because of the grace and love of God.

Repentance is not a dirty word. In fact, it is a gift of grace. It is God demonstrating His love and favor towards saints and sinners alike. It is an opportunity from God for sinners to receive Christ and be saved from wrath, and for the saints to believe Christ truth and be empowered to live victoriously. God sent Jesus to give us the gift of repentance. The Bible says, "*Repent, then, and turn to God, so that your sins may be wiped out, that times of refreshing may come from the Lord.*"[17] When we cry out to God for mercy, as King David, God refreshes and restores the joy of our salvation because of His unfailing love. He is generous in love, abundant in mercy and blots out our transgressions.

Jesus said, "*For God did not send His Son into the world to condemn the world, but to save the world through Him.*"[18] God's kindness is intended to lead you to repentance.[19] Child of God, when God calls you to repent,

He is not condemning you. He is pleading with you as a loving Father and calls you to repentance that is available to the vilest sinner by grace through faith. Repentance simply means to change your mind or rethink your position on a matter and keep moving in the right direction.

In Mark 1:15, Jesus was not yelling or threatening people. He was lovingly proclaiming the good news, telling them to change their minds and rethink their position about the kingdom and how to enter in. He wanted them to believe the Good News that the Kingdom was within reach, and they could enter it immediately through faith in Him.

What about you? Do you need to rethink your view of God, salvation, sin, righteousness, or repentance? Then do so. Accept God's gift of repentance today and ask the Holy Spirit to begin renewing your mind with the Word. That's God's way to salvation, and that's the way to a victorious life in Him.

ENDNOTES

1. Ten Boom, Corrie. "Corrie Ten Boom Quotes." BrainyQuotes, Web. March 25, 2017, https://www.brainyquote.com/quotes/quotes/c/corrietenb381187.html.

2. Romans 3:23

3. Luke 11:4

4. Micah 7:18-19

5. Hebrews 12:5

6. Psalm 30:1-3

7. "Anastasis," BibleHub.com, Strong's Greek Dictionary, Web. March 26, 2017, http://biblehub.com/greek/386.html.

8. Philippians 3:10

9. "Skandalizó, skandalo," BibleHub.com, Strong's Greek Dictionary, Web. March 26, 2017, http://biblehub.com/greek/4624.html.

10. Bevere, John, "Bait of Satan: Living Free from the Deadly Trap of Offense," (New York: Charisma House 2004) 6.

11. Matthew 16:21

12. Luke 17:1

13. Psalm 91:2

14. Mark 1:14-15

15. Thayer, J. H. 1958. Greek-English Lexicon of the New Testament. Edinburgh: T. & T. Clark.

16. 2 Corinthians 7:10

17. Acts 3:19

18. John 3:17

19. Romans 2:4

Chapter 5

FAITH, GRACE, AND PRAYER

"Faith is taking the first step even when
you don't see the whole staircase."
Dr. Martin Luther King[1]

"Now faith is confidence in what we hope for and assurance about what we do not see."[2] Faith is real. Faith is the substance of things hoped for, the evidence of things not seen. The things we expect to receive from God by faith. Faith is taking God at His Word. Believing in God's power, wisdom and goodness, and believing that He rewards the people who earnestly seek Him. *"Without faith it is impossible to please God."*[3]

We put our faith in the promises of God, in the truth He's revealed in our hearts through His Word and by the Holy Spirit. The promises are to those who believe and have learned to access them by faith. The promise depends entirely on confident trust in an unseen God. My mantra became *"My ears had heard of you but now my eyes have seen you."*[4]

Faith doesn't make sense in the natural realm because faith cannot be seen or understood when situations beyond our control require us to believe beyond what we can see with our natural eyes. The Amplified Version translates it this way, "*NOW FAITH is the assurance (the confirmation, the title deed) of the things [we] hope for, being the proof of things [we] do not see and the conviction of their reality [faith perceiving as real fact what is not revealed to the senses].*"[5] Faith is the proof of the things we are hoping for, seeing as real what is not yet evident in the natural realm. In Hebrews, the ancients noted Abraham, Isaac, Moses, all had faith; otherwise they would not have seen nor been able to do the things God asked of them.

God is always bigger than our problems when we see through the eyes of faith. When I didn't understand God's inner workings in my life, my faith was challenged. I had to learn to face and confront my fears, failures, negative habits, and other hindrances that prevented me from living in the fullness of God. God has never failed me—no, not one time.

God will reveal His power over your circumstances. In difficult times, you may be stretched beyond your ability to endure. It is during those times we learn to totally depend on Him. Many times, I came to the end of my rope. Each time God provided a way for me to stand under the pressure. He intervened and made my affliction work for Him rather than against me when I looked beyond my circumstances through the eyes of faith. His plan was to bring me out with a mighty hand and outstretched arm.

It didn't matter whether I lost my house, my car, my job or ministry, or suffered a personal attack from Satan. God's grace always sustained me regardless of my inability to see my way through with my natural eyes. I experienced the power and grace of God overruling my circumstances every time. God's grace is sufficient.[6] His grace is all you need. It provides you with sufficient knowledge, wisdom and understanding, both in the physical and spiritual realms. His grace supplies you with sufficient strength to stand against the onslaught of the enemy and do all He asked you to do.

When you believe for something, don't be moved by what you see, what you hear, what you feel or how long it takes for it to materialize. Stand firm on God's Word. Take the limits off and walk by faith. Meditate on the scriptures. Speak to your mountains and command them to move in Jesus Name!

Unbelief is your greatest enemy. Unbelief causes circumstances to appear larger than they may be. It becomes a giant that throws you off track. Early in my walk and ministry, the Lord revealed to me not to allow unbelief to become the sin that entraps me. Know that when you walk by faith you will overcome the enemy efforts to derail you. You will be able to rise above what you see and believe for those things that are accessed by faith.

Walk by Faith, Not by Sight

Jesus said in Matthew 19:26, "*With man this is impossible, but with God all things are possible.*" Faith arises in your life when you see with the eyes of faith. We may not see in the natural the things God has promised, yet we continue to see and believe with the eyes of faith. The eyes of faith are God's eyes. They see from God's perspective. Seeing with spiritual eyes the things God has promised. They allow you to see the invisible. They allow you to see the unseen. There is no darkness when you see with the eyes of faith because you trust in Him.

In Ephesians, Paul prayed, "*that the eyes of your heart may be enlightened in order that you may know the hope to which he has called you, the riches of his glorious inheritance in his holy people, and his incomparably great power for us who believe. That power is the same as the mighty strength.*"[7]

The eyes of our heart are the very center and core of our being. The Holy Spirit will enlighten our hearts with God's truth so that we will know and cherish the hope to which God has called us.

At times, I've struggled with my faith. There were times I thought I had missed God because of what was happening in my life. I sensed my hope was fading while waiting for the manifestation of His promises. I felt sick at heart. *"Hope deferred makes the heart sick."*[8] However, what's happening in the natural was only temporary. The supernatural is what is real. God is faithful to keep His promises. When God's promises seemed so far away. I would pray that God would *"Open my eyes that I may see wonderful things in your law."*[9] During times of crisis your faith will be challenged. Perspective is important. We base our decisions and how we live our lives on how we see things. God is continually teaching me to see with new eyes, challenging my faith, and challenging me to see from His perspective and not my own. When faced with challenges, draw near to God with a sincere heart in full confidence of faith, holding fast the confession of our hope without wavering.

God doesn't expect you to be perfect, just stay in faith. Keep believing what He has promised even when it has not yet manifested in the natural. Don't let the enemy throw you off track by looking at your natural circumstances, or delayed promises causing you to doubt God's Word. God uses His delays to teach you to trust Him. Keep believing what has been spoken in your heart. In doing so, you will be able to rise above what you see and believe for those things that you cannot see as those who have seen the invisible.[10] You have the same capacity as the heroes of faith to see beyond the natural into the supernatural realm things your eyes have not seen nor ears heard what God has prepared for you. *"What no eye has seen, what no ear has heard, and what no human mind has conceived"* —the things God has prepared for those who love him."[11]

Learn to rest in Him. Willingness to rest in Him assures your destiny and purpose. Allow His peace to govern your heart, and He will direct your pursuits according to His good will and pleasure. Don't look at what is happening with others. Keep your eyes fixed on Jesus. He did not bring you this far to forsake you now. Keep pressing into Him to reach your destiny. The testing of your faith is producing something greater in you.

At times, I didn't understand the things God would speak to me through the Holy Spirit. The Lord revealed to me, it was a seed! Don't worry if people don't believe or receive you. As a young believer, this was a struggle for me during seasons of preparation because in my heart I so wanted people to see what I was seeing in the spirit realm. As things begin to unfold, He would remind me of all He had spoken, stirring up my faith to keep pressing forward. Today, I am seeing the manifestation of what was promised long ago.

Regardless of what others believe, continue to believe what has been deposited in your heart/spirit. Allow God to lead you. He will fulfill His promises and transition you into the place He has prepared for you. You don't have the ability to do it yourself. Transition does not allow you to stay in same place. Throughout Jesus' ministry He transitioned people from one state to another. If we are not careful we miss God in the transition because when we take our eyes off Him because of lack of trust, lack of faith, or fear of the unknown.

I remember in the beginning of my walk with the Lord I heard the call to full-time ministry, yet I couldn't do anything to get there myself. Then suddenly after a season of preparation, He transitioned me. The opportunity presented itself for me to leave my full-time job at a time went the organization was down-sizing. So, I took the leap of faith, transitioned and never looked back.

Transition is the process, or a period of changing from one state or condition to another. The movement, passage, or change from one position, state, stage to another.[12] Now this is good, because it was far beyond my understanding of what God would do. It happened suddenly. One moment I was in one place, and then the next thing I knew, I had been repositioned into full time ministry. Only God could do what was done to get me there. I am in new season of transition, but it won't be the same. There are new opportunities, new doors that are opening for me that require a new level of faith. One thing I know is it will happen suddenly according to God's divine will and purpose.

During seasons of transition, Satan will try to confuse you. He will try to convince you that you made a mistake. God will teach you how to trust and wait on Him. Waiting is a time of testing. Throughout this time of testing when doors were closed, the Lord said some things to me that surprised me.

> He said, "I know what you will do, but do you? You need to learn how to trust ME! You need to learn how not to quit. Don't look at where I have you now. Many think you have failed and will never recover, but I am dealing with you. I AM dealing with your faith. I AM restoring you. And it will not happen until I AM ready. I need you to trust Me at another level. You took your eyes off Me for a moment. You almost slipped, but I caught you. I know it has been hard, but I have been with you all the way. Be careful what you allow the enemy to talk to you about. His task is to magnify things to make them appear to be something they are not. Your faith began to fail you when you stopped trusting Me and began to trust what others were saying, including the voice of unbelief."

This is when the Lord began to warn me about overcoming the spirit of unbelief. The Word that we hear will only profit when it is mixed with faith.[13] Unbelief hinders you from trusting the voice of the Lord and trusting in His provisions. When faith is released, the anointing shows up, and the supernatural takes place.

Seeing with Eagle Eyes

You must have "eagle eyes" to discern a matter. You must have clear vision. There may be times when your vision is cloudy because of how you feel. That's why you cannot depend on your feelings. You must discern a matter with eagle's eyes of faith. Don't trust your natural eyes and what you see physically. Your natural eyes can deceive you. Seek the heart of God on a matter and do what He tells you. Allow Him to bring to pass those things that you desire.

Once I received a beautiful vision of soaring on eagle's wings high above the snowcapped mountains. I came to understand God was delivering me, carrying me over my circumstances, and drawing me closer to Him. I live in an area where eagles are present. Seeing them soar with beauty and grace is a spectacular sight and reminds me of how God said He carried the children of Israel on eagle's wings.[14]

Eagles glide without flapping their wings. Their wings are spread straight out, and they are literally soaring with perfect ease on the wind currents. They have strong vision, with an ability to focus on objects up to three miles away. When an eagle sights his prey, he will not move his focus from the prey until he successfully captures it. To succeed, we must have a clear vision and remain focused, no matter what obstacles we face.

The eagle eye is among the strongest in the animal kingdom, with an eyesight estimated at four to eight times stronger than that of the average human.[15] As the eagle descends from the sky to attack its prey, the muscles in the eyes continuously adjust the curvature of the eyeballs to maintain sharp focus and accurate perception throughout the approach and attack.[16] We may have to adjust our focus at times to keep our eyes on the prize of the high calling of God.

God brought the children of Israel out of Egypt to carry them to Himself. Yet they didn't trust Him and wandered in the desert for forty years instead. We must learn to be led by the Holy Spirit daily so we can fully accomplish everything God has called us to do. The Holy Spirit will lead and guide you in the direction you should go. The challenge is in learning to wait on the Lord until we catch the wind of His Spirit.

Trusting in God's Timing

Have you ever been waiting for something that just seem to be delayed? What if you have to "wait on God"? At times, you may be praying and believing for something and maybe even get to the place where you are not sure that God even hears your prayers anymore. I have been here a few times. You wait, you hope, you pray, you become anxious and fear that it will never happen. My dear sister, God's timing is perfect, just as all His ways are perfect. His timing is never early, and it's never late. He is in complete control of everything and everyone. No event in history has put so much as a wrinkle in the timing of God's eternal plan, which He designed before the foundation of the world.

Although I don't consider myself impatient, there have been times when I've become anxious while waiting for the manifestation of His promises. There have been times I've wondered when He will come through. It is during times of waiting I learned to calm my anxious thoughts and spiraling emotions. It was during those times God was cultivating patience in me. I could choose to run ahead of Him and try to make things happen myself, or I could wait patiently for the manifestation of His promise.

Why is that important? Patience is a spiritual fruit and God is pleased when we display patience. He is good to those who confidently wait for Him. Our patience, or lack thereof, often reveals how much we trust in His timing. God operates according to His perfect timing, not ours. When we wait on the LORD, expecting and hoping in Him, we gain new strength and renew our strength.[17] The eagle represents a sign of strength. God renews our strength like that of the eagle.

We also learn to trust in God's timing. When you trust Him with all our heart, and forgo leaning to your own understanding, the Holy Spirit will guide into God's will. One thing is certain—before God moves, we will have to wait. Waiting for answers and the manifestation of His promises is a fact of life. The question is not if we'll wait, but rather how we'll wait. Will we wait passively or expectantly? When we wait expectantly our hearts are full of hope, expecting our prayers to be answered at any moment. We wake up every morning expecting God's answer. We may wait and wait, but suddenly what we've been waiting for happens. Hallelujah! *"I remain confident of this: I will see the goodness of the LORD in the land of the living."*[18]

How often do you become frustrated while waiting and take matters into our own hands? It's never a good idea to try to accomplish God's plan in your own way and your own timing. God's plans come complete with His methods and His timing, and when we try to interfere with that, it messes everything up. *"Wait for the LORD; be strong and take heart and wait for the LORD."* [19] What has God promised you today? Wait for it expectantly.

Rahab, Heroine of Faith

There are several amazing stories in the Bible of women whose faith bought about some miraculous changes in their lives and in the lives of others. Rahab is one of those women. Her name is recorded in Hebrews 11:31 because her faith.

Rahab is a young Canaanite prostitute of the city of Jericho. She is an unlikely candidate for a heroine of the faith. Rahab was born outside of the covenant, yet she believed that the God of the children of Israel was a faithful God. She is best known for helping Joshua's spies escape from Jericho after they sneaked into the city. What amazes me about Rahab is her faith, even when she had no idea what the outcome would be. Rahab allows two Israelite spies to stay in her home and, by doing so, risks her life. Why? She heard about the exploits of Israel and how God had done miracles for the nation. Rahab remembered stories she heard of them and their God, such as how He opened the Red Sea before them. Though her faith is never mentioned in the story, twice she describes the anxiety she and her fellow citizens felt. She obviously put her trust in the God of Israel, and that is why Rahab is listed in Jesus' genealogy. She is willing to put her life at risk by hiding the two spies of Israel. She is a true heroine of the faith.

The Syrophoenician Woman: A Woman of Great Faith

Another woman of great faith that's not often spoke about is the Syrophoenician woman. The story of the Syrophoenician woman found in the Book of Matthew and Mark is one of the most intriguing accounts of great faith and healing in the Gospels.

The Book of Matthew says Jesus leaves Galilee and goes north to the region of Tyre and Sidon. A certain woman comes to Jesus, crying out, *"Lord, Son of David, have mercy on me! My daughter is demon-possessed and suffering terribly."*[20]

The woman is a Gentile, of Syrophoenician birth. Her and her daughter's names are not known. What we do know is she was a mother grieving because of her daughter's demoniac affliction. She wants Jesus to cast the devil out of her daughter. Jesus' initial response is silence. What do the disciples do? They ask Jesus to send her away. Eventually, Jesus responds to the woman by saying, *"I was sent only to the lost sheep of Israel."*[21]

I'm fascinated that this nameless woman has the boldness, courage, and resolve to approach Jesus to ask for something she does not have a right to because she is not a part of the covenant. Her persistence pays off in the end. She kneels before Jesus and asked Him to help her. Jesus replies to her,

"It is not right to take the children's bread and toss it to the dogs."[22] What? Jesus calls this woman a dog? I know some of you would be offended if Jesus called you a dog. But, this woman is determined not to take "no" for an answer. With remarkable insight and persistence, she replies:

> *"Yes, it is, Lord…Even the dogs eat the crumbs that fall from their master's table." Then Jesus said to her, "Woman, you have great faith! Your request is granted." And her daughter was healed at that moment.*[23]

The distress and trouble of her family brings this woman to Christ, and because of her faith, Jesus grants her request for a miracle. Is Jesus calling her a dog? Absolutely not. This lady has great spiritual insight. She isn't asking Jesus to alter the way He carries out the plan of God. She is simply asking for a crumb, scrap or portion for the deliverance of her child.

It's important to note that Jesus isn't insulting a desperate woman seeking the health and welfare of her family. Jesus came to the lost house of Israel, bringing the Gospel to the Jews first. In Romans 1:16 Paul says, *"For I am not ashamed of the gospel, because it is the power of God that brings salvation to everyone who believes: first to the Jew, then to the Gentile."* That was God's plan, to offer salvation to the Jews first.

What a relevant message for today. I believe the Holy Spirit encouraged me to include her story because of her great faith and to reveal to you that no matter what walk of life you come from, no matter what position you hold in society, Jesus has mercy stored up for you and will look upon you favorably if you put your trust and confidence in Him. Psalm 31:19 says, *"How abundant are the good things that you have stored up for those who fear you, that you bestow in the sight of all, on those who take refuge in you."* Jesus blesses this woman before the world.

Grace That Is Simply Amazing

Grace is ours. God offers you grace through His Son, Jesus Christ. Grace is the undeserved, unearned favor of God that gives you access to the power of God for everything you need for life and godliness. Not only are we saved by grace, but we are to grow in grace.

God demonstrated His love and favored us *"while we were still sinners."*[24] We didn't deserve God's favor, but God loved us so much that He sent His Son to die for us so that we might have access to His grace through faith in Him. We can come to the throne of grace with boldness, receive His mercy, and find grace to help in our times of need.

Everything we receive from God comes through His grace. The Bible says we are saved through grace, we believe through grace, we obey by grace, we stand firm in grace, and we receive our inheritance by grace.[25] God's grace gives us the power to believe and obey. It is not something we do of ourselves. So many people are living in condemnation because they don't have a revelation that grace gives them access to the power of God to obey His will. The Lord freely lavishes His grace upon you so that you may live for Him and with Him forever.

God's grace motivates us to serve Him and sustains us in our trials. Paul writes: *"The love of Christ compels us!"*[26] There is nothing like the freedom that comes through grace. God's grace is so amazing!

Unexpected Connection, Unexpected Grace

It was high noon on a hot day. Jesus, tired from traveling, chooses to rest at Jacob's well near the town of Sychar, while waiting for His disciples to go into town for food. An unnamed Samaritan woman comes to draw water at a well. She hates facing others because the Jews despise her people, and she is an outcast looked down upon even by her own people. This woman is ostracized and marked as immoral, an unmarried woman living openly with the sixth in a series of men. She could not have guessed the surprise she was about to encounter that day.

An Offer She Couldn't Refuse

Grace often comes as a surprise when we are least expecting it. When the Samaritan woman appears with clay jar in hand, Jesus makes a simple request: "*Will you give me a drink?*"[27] He had been sitting there, tired and thirsty from His day of traveling. Shocked and a bit startled, she wonders how He can ask her for a drink of water. She is a woman, and a Samaritan, whom the Jews despised. Asking for water would make Him ceremonially unclean. She says to him, "*You are a Jew and I am a Samaritan woman. How can you ask me for a drink?' Jesus answered her, 'If you knew the gift of God and who it is that asks you for a drink, you would have asked him, and he would have given you living water.*"[28]

Jesus tells her He can give her "*living water*" so that she will never thirst again; an irresistible offering. This polite but fearless woman points out the obvious: "*You have nothing to draw with and the well is deep. Where can you get this living water?*"[29] Her natural curiosity prompts her to ask questions.

To quench her spiritual thirst, the Lord first confesses the truth about plain water: "*Everyone who drinks this water will be thirsty again.*"[30] Then Jesus makes a bold promise: "*Whoever drinks the water I give him will never thirst.*"[31] The Samaritan woman wants whatever He is offering, but only so she can avoid returning to the well for water. If we're honest, in eagerness to satisfy our physical desires, we overlook our spiritual needs. Jesus is offering the free gift of grace through faith.

Jesus Knows the Complexities of Our Lives

Jesus then tells her, "*Go, call your husband and come back.*"[32] Not an odd request, since women couldn't converse alone with a man in a public place. But Jesus' request is more about uncovering truth than about following society's rules.

When she confesses, "*I have no husband,*" Jesus affirms her answer, then gently exposes her sin: "*The fact is, you have had five husbands, and the man you now have is not your husband.*"[33] To the woman's surprise, Jesus reveals she had had five husbands and is living with a man she is not married to.

After this amazing encounter with Jesus, the Samaritan woman runs into town to tell everyone about her encounter. "*Many of the Samaritans from that town believed in him because of the woman's testimony,* "*He told me everything I ever did." When the Samaritans came to him, they urged him to stay with them, and he stayed two days.*"[34]

Perhaps Jesus knows there is a longing in her heart that she hadn't yet expressed. She needs redemption; someone to rescue her from the turmoil of her life. We know she is touched in a powerful way because the accounts show her story convinced many Samaritans to believe in Jesus as their Savior.

Perhaps many of you are like the woman at the well. We come burdened with the shame of our past, afraid of what others might think or say if they knew about our past. Yet Jesus is not like that. Praise God! He met this woman at the deepest, darkest point of her life and changed her life forever.

The Lord had one more nugget He wanted me to share with you about how He changed this woman's life forever. While attending the Women of the Frontlines World Convention 2017, I learned through Dr. Brian Simmons, author of *The Passion Translation*, that this woman had a name. What was her name? Jesus knew her name. Her name was "Photini." Even though they'd never met, He knew everything about her. He knew the day she was born, how many hairs were on her head, and every detail of her mysterious past. He knew her, because He was the One who created her. Not only that, she occupies a place of honor among the apostles. She received baptism, along with her five sisters and her two sons.[35] You may feel like an outcast but, no matter who you are, Jesus will always go out of His way for you.

Naked and Not Ashamed

In Genesis 2, before the fall in the Garden, Adam and his wife Eve were both naked, and they were not ashamed. They were not overcome by guilt or fear, nor were they driven by condemnation. They were hiding behind nothing. They were naked. They were in constant fellowship and communion with God. They walked together in perfect harmony.

You know what happened. The serpent deceived Eve. Deception entered the world. After the fall, they hid from the Lord God among the trees of the garden because they were afraid and naked. Genesis 3:7 says, "*Then the eyes of both of them were opened, and they realized they were naked; so they sewed fig leaves together and made coverings for themselves.*"

Guilt and shame is like a weight. When we carry around guilt and shame day after day, they begin to weigh us down. They take a toll on our health, and causes emotional damage to our soul. They affect every area of our lives. God longs to heal us of guilt and shame. He offers healing for our weary souls. Guilt and shame can literally weigh us down. What do you carry around that weighs you down? That makes you want to hide from God and the world?

What did Jesus do to shame? He despised it! Jesus despised the shame, "*For the joy set before him he endured the cross, scorning its shame, and sat down at the right hand of the throne of God.*"[36]

Jesus despised the shame of the agony of the cross, knowing He was about to take on the sins of the world! He knew something greater was about to take place. He knew the shame of the cross was fleeting and insignificant in light of God's plan to redeem mankind.

When guilt and shame threatens to expose, humiliate, or devalue you, despise those false whispers, have the courage and boldness to endure it, because it is ultimately inconsequential in light of God's glory. God has placed lavish promises in my heart. And letting go of guilt and shame, and taking hold of grace is where it all begins.

Don't allow the enemy to accuse you of what God has already forgiven! Don't let him fool you into thinking that Jesus' death on the cross was not enough. Take hold of what Jesus has already taken hold of for you. Romans 8:1-2 says, "*Therefore, there is now no condemnation for those who are in Christ Jesus, because through Christ Jesus the law of the Spirit who gives life has set you free from the law of sin and death.*"

Hebrews 12:1 tells us to "*throw off everything that hinders and the sin that so easily entangles*" so we can "*run with perseverance the race marked out for us, fixing our eyes on Jesus, the pioneer and perfector of faith.*"[37] Shame leaves you vulnerable to Satan's schemes. Regardless of your condition, anyone who believes or trusts in Christ will not be put to shame or disgraced. Psalm 34:5 says, "*Those who look to him are radiant; their faces are never covered with shame.*"

Creating Space for God

Jesus knew how important it was to create space for God in his life and to take time to develop and grow in His relationship to the Father. No matter how busy He was, Jesus always made the time to pull away from the crowds and the disciples to be with the Father in prayer. If He didn't, He knew that He would never be able to accomplish the Father's will in His life. If Jesus was intentional about creating space for God, then it stands to reason that we must do the same.

What does it mean to create space for God? Following Jesus is about having a personal relationship with Him. I don't have the ability to do what God has asked of me without Him. My best efforts cannot accomplish what only God Himself can do. My life is hidden in Christ. So, like Jesus, it is a must for me to create space for Him in my life to develop and grow in my relationship with the Father.

We must carve out time for Him every day. All we need is an uninterrupted portion of time dedicated to prayer, and an open heart. Come with boldness before the throne of grace and spend time with the one who loves you eternally.[38] The Spirit of God moves powerfully in our lives when we spend time in the presence of the Lord.

Don't allow distractions to take precedence in your life. There is something special about slowing down, turning off distractions, and opening your heart and life to God through His Word.[39]

I have not found nothing to be richer or more rewarding than meditating on the Word of God. Meditating creates a space for Him to transform our minds and awaken our souls to more of Him. Carve out time to read God's Word every single day. Reading His Word should be a deeply personal time with God in which you are learning and soaking in His truth.

Take time to get alone with Him in the "*secret place*," to be strengthened in your identity as a son or daughter. David understood his identity in Christ because he spent time alone with God. When we are alone with God, we draw closer to Him and get to know Him in a deeper more intimate way. God desires "alone time" with you. He wants a personal relationship with you. When we desire to know Him intimately, we seek Him early and spend time with Him because His love is better than life.[40] When I spend time alone with God, I experience a freedom to express myself to Him and allow Him to speak with me through His Word and the Holy Spirit. It is a unique privilege to spend time alone with God and realize how much He loves you. A great way to start is by slowing down and acknowledging Him in the stillness and quiet. He declared in Psalm 46:10, "*Be still, and know that I am God.*" A life of faith is strengthened when you spend time with God. Make time and space to enjoy quiet time with Him when you can focus your thoughts and prayers. You will bring a since of calm and order into your home while enhancing your spiritual life.

Daily prayer is also important. Prayer is a time to praise God, confess sins, ask for forgiveness, and present your needs and worries to Him. And attending church is also important. Consistently gathering together with a body of believers is an opportunity to grow in your love and commitment to God and your desire to put him first in your life.

Praise Is a Powerful Weapon

Praise, according to the Scriptures, is an act of our will that flows out of an awe and reverence for our Creator. Praise gives glory to God and opens you up to a deeper union with Him. It turns your attention from your problems and onto the nature and character of God Himself. The results can fill you with peace and contentment and transform your outlook on life. Very simply, we praise God because He is worthy of our praise. He is the Alpha and Omega, the Beginning and the End, the King of Kings and Lord of Lords. He is our Creator, Provider, Healer, Redeemer, Judge, Defender, and much more.

Praise is a powerful instrument. Amid everyday life circumstances and times of spiritual warfare, we sometimes forget to praise, or struggle to pray. In 2 Chronicles 20, as King Jehoshaphat and all who live in Judah and Jerusalem began to sing and praise, the Lord set ambushes against their enemies until they were defeated.

This is one of the wonders of praise. Praises to God bring down His presence and makes Him to show Himself as the Almighty. King Jehoshaphat and his people organized a choir according to God's directive, and they began to praise God even when the enemies were already very close to them. Three nations rose against them, yet they believed that by praise they would have victory because God said so.

One thing you should not do is focus on the seemingly overwhelming forces of darkness coming against your life. When you do, you give the devil the advantage. I recall a season of tremendous warfare in my family when I could hardly get a praise out of my mouth. It seemed as if no matter what I did, Satan was attempting to completely wipe me out. What did I do? I began to praise Him in the middle of my circumstances. Praise agrees with God's unchanging nature and disagrees with the lies of the enemy. When we praise God in the middle of the battles, it's like having a double-edged sword in our mouth. *"May the praise of God be in their mouths and a double-edged sword in their hands."*[41]

True praise is a response to His very nature and agrees with who the Bible declares Him to be. Praise elevates your perspective, causing you to see from God's vantage point. *"I will lift up my eyes to the hills, from where does my help come? My help comes from the Lord, who made heaven and earth."*[42]

Praise Him because He is good. Praise Him for all He has done and all He is going to do. Praise Him for all of creation and for giving you the opportunity to live a life of freedom and joy! Praise brings us into the safety of God's Presence. We are to, *"give thanks in all circumstances; for this is God's will for you in Christ Jesus."*[43]

Cultivating a Heart of Worship

Worship is about encountering God in a personal, transforming way. John 4:21:24 tells us that God is Spirit and that true worship is seeking God in spirit and in truth. Jesus says that a time is coming, and as a matter of fact is already here, when it will not matter where you go to worship. The Father is looking for those who will worship Him in spirit and in truth. God is a Spirit, and those who worship Him must do it out of their spirits, their true selves, in adoration of Him.

Worship can be as simple as having an attitude of devotion, gratitude, and obedience towards God. It can also involve verbally expressing the greatness of God and your commitment to him. This can be spoken or sung. Worship may be your own spontaneous words, or they may come from a written text, such as decrees. You can worship alone, with family or friends, or in church fellowship with many people.

God wants you to worship Him, not just for His sake, but for yours as well. When we worship God, we are reminded of His power and love, and this strengthens and revives your faith in Him. When we worship and focus on God and His greatness, we get a genuine perspective on life in line with His truth.

Worship is not just about saying words or thinking wonderful thoughts about God. As with prayer, when we worship God, we are connecting with Him spiritually. Worship can also be expressed when we are obedient to God in practical ways. The Father is seeking true worshippers, those who worship Him in spirit because they know the truth. They have experienced the power of the blood as well as His love, forgiveness, grace, and mercy.

ENDNOTES

1. "Martin Luther King, Jr. Quotes." *Brainy Quotes*. Web. March 26, 2017, https://www.brainyquote.com/quotes/quotes/m/martinlu-th105087.html.

2. Hebrews 11:1

3. Hebrews 11:6

4. Job 42:5

5. Hebrews 11:1 AMP

6. 2 Corinthians 12:9

7. Ephesians 1:18-19

8. Proverbs 13:12

9. Psalm 119:18

10. Hebrews 11:27

11. 1 Corinthians 2:9

12. "Transition." *Merriam-Webster.com*. Merriam-Webster, n.d. Web. 7 July 2017.

13. Hebrews 4:2

14. Exodus 19:4

15. *"Eagle eye." Wikipedia.org*, Web. February 17, 2017, https://en.wikipedia.org/wiki/Eagle_eye.

16. Ibid.

17. Isaiah 40:31

18. Psalm 27:13-14

19. Ibid.

20. Matthew 15:21-28

21. Ibid.

22. Ibid.

23. Ibid.

24. Romans 5:8

25. Acts 15:11, Acts 18:27, Acts 20:32, Romans 5:1-2

26. 2 Corinthians 5:14

27. John 4:7-40

28. Ibid.

29. Ibid.

30. Ibid.

31. Ibid.

32. Ibid.

33. Ibid.

34. Ibid.

35. Catafygiotu, Eva, *OrthodoxChristianInfo*, "*St Photini, The Samaritan Woman*," Adapted from Saints and Sisterhood: The lives of forty-eight Holy Women, Web. May 8, 2017, http://www.orthodoxchristian.info/pages/photini.htm.

36. Hebrews 12:2

37. Ibid.

38. Hebrews 4:16

39. Hebrews 4:12

40. Psalm 63:1-3

41. Psalm 149:6

42. Psalm 121:1-2

43. 1 Thessalonians 5:18

Chapter 6

OBEDIENCE IS BETTER THAN SACRIFICE

*"You are my friends if you do what I command. I no longer
call you servants, because a servant does not know his master's
business. Instead, I have called you friends, for everything that I
learned from my Father I have made known to you."*
John 15:14-15

When you choose a life of obedience, you become God's friend. God called Abraham friend because he believed God, and it was credited to him as righteousness. The term "friend" conveys a sense of closeness and trust. Living a life of integrity and obedience to God always brings blessings and has the potential to positively impact others.

Obedience in everyday life pleases God. In 1 Samuel 15, the Bible tells the story of a man who thinks God won't mind if he is a little disobedient, if he makes a sacrifice to God instead of following Samuel's instructions.

King Saul thinks God will not mind if he doesn't do everything the way God says. He thinks he can give God a sacrifice instead of his full obedience. Saul is wrong. When Samuel learns that Saul disobeyed his instructions, he informs Saul that God has rejected him as king because of his disobedience.

> *"Does the LORD delight in burnt offerings and sacrifices as much as in obeying the LORD? To obey is better than sacrifice, and to heed is better than the fat of rams. For rebellion //is like the sin of divination, and arrogance like the evil of idolatry. Because you have rejected the word of the Lord, he has rejected you as king."*[1]

Saul thinks he can substitute sacrifice, or worship, for obedience. Obedience is very important to God, and He attaches a lot of benefits to it. *"If they obey and serve Him, they will spend their days in prosperity and their years in pleasure. To obey is better than sacrifice,"*[2]

God's Pathway of Brokenness

> *"The LORD is close to the brokenhearted and saves those who are crushed in spirit." – Psalm 34:18*

Broken and blessed don't seem to fit together—at least not in my mind, and I would have never considered brokenness as a blessing until I went through it myself. What I realized in my seasons of brokenness is that it truly is a blessing. When you think of how earth-shattering life's blows can be, can we believe God will bring good out of our most heartbreaking and devastating crises? Dr. Charles Stanley in *The Blessings of Brokenness* says, "It's difficult to discern the blessing in the midst of brokenness."[3] How true. We must trust God's plan for us and look for what He is teaching us in those challenging times.

Shattered Hopes and Dreams

We all have dreams. Dreams for our children, dreams for our marriage, dreams for our lives. So, what do you do when one or all of those dreams gets shattered? How do you recover and go on?

I think one of the most difficult things in life to deal with are shattered dreams, and we all have them—broken relationships, broken dreams, and broken lives. When I think of something broken, I think of something shattered and irreparable, like a broken glass or jar that is impossible to repair. But did you know that God uses the pain of brokenness and shattered dreams to help us discover our desire for Him. You are never too broken for restoration. You are never too shattered for repair.

The story of Ruth is one of the most powerful portrayals of amazing love and extravagant grace born out of a season of brokenness. It puts pressing contemporary issues at the forefront, such as brokenness and loss, the plight of women in the world, widowhood, poverty and wealth, and the radical courage and good that comes from living as God's child in this fallen world. This book shows that God responds to His people's cry and views God through the eyes of a woman.

Naomi loses everything: home, husband, sons, and her livelihood. She cries out in her grief, not knowing that God had a plan of restoration. God provides for Naomi and Ruth, two widows with little prospects for a future. The story reveals the magnitude of God's grace. It shows the loving, faithful nature of God. He accepts Ruth as one of His chosen people and honors her with a role in creating the family line into which His appointed king, David, and later His Son, Jesus, would be born.

Beauty in Brokenness

"And provide for those who grieve in Zion—to bestow on them a crown of beauty instead of ashes, the oil of joy instead of mourning, and a garment of praise instead of a spirit of despair."
– Isaiah 61:3

I want to share another story that touched me deeply when I was faced with seemly impossible circumstances. One of my favorite stories in the Bible is about Hagar, Sarai's Egyptian maidservant. We all know the story of Ruth and Naomi and how in the midst of shattered dreams, God steps in and restores their lives. What about Hagar, seldom mentioned, yet a powerful example of God's redemptive love and extravagant grace?

There are three main characters in this story: Abram, a husband who seeks to keep peace, and his two wives. Sarai and Hagar. Sarai, a desperate, aged housewife who believes she cannot have a son, finds another way to accomplish her desire, and encourages a young, enslaved Egyptian girl named Hagar to sleep with Abram to bear him a son. As a slave, she has no status in the community.

In Genesis 16, God promises Abram that he would have a son. After waiting ten years in Canaan, Sarai takes the initiative and urges Abraham to sleep with her maidservant. In ancient Near Eastern practice, giving another woman to your husband to bear a child is common and acceptable.[4] If Hagar had a baby, the baby would count as Sarai's child.

Abram agrees to Sarai's request and slept with Hagar. Can you imagine that? Once Hagar realizes she is pregnant, she begins to despise her mistress. Sarai blames Abram. Abram tells Sarai to do with Hagar what she thinks is best. Sarai responds to this contempt by dealing harshly with Hagar. So, Hagar flees Sarai's oppression. After fleeing, the angel of the Lord finds Hagar by a spring in the desert on the way to Shur. The road through Shur was the road to Egypt. So, Hagar is on her way home, on her way to freedom.

Hagar is pregnant, alone, and in despair, when the angel of the Lord finds her and asks, "*Where have you come from, and where are you going*?" Hagar knows that this is God talking to her through this angel. She answers, "*I'm running away from my mistress Sarai,*"[5] When I read this, I think of all the young women who have been pregnant, alone and in despair. The Lord sees your pain and your struggle. He will not forsake you.

Scripture reminds us that God is omniscient. He knows and cares about every detail of our lives even down to when we lose a single hair. In Hagar's case, God knows she is a slave, and He knows how slavery has dehumanized Hagar. Nonetheless, God tells Hagar, "*Go back to your mistress and submit to her.*"[6] What would you do if God told you to return like Hagar? Would you obey Him?

God comes alongside Hagar to console, comfort, and encourage her. So, what does God promise Hagar to encourage and comfort her? He promises her a son and a multitude of descendants. Hagar names the Lord who spoke to her *El Roi*, meaning "You are the God who sees me," for she said, "*I have now seen the One who sees me.*"[7] We see God breaking through Hagar's shattered reality with a promise. How many times have you found yourself in a painful situation and wanted to run away from your problems thinking things will get better? When you pray to *El Roi*, you are praying to the one who knows everything about you, and He responds to your shattered reality with a promise of hope and a future.

In my own journey, there have been times I had to choose to remain in a place that my flesh was screaming to be released from, struggling to find worth amid pain and despair. Separated with two young sons, I found myself broken and feeling hopeless. Who could I turn to but the God who sees me in the pit of despair and loves me just the same? I stuck it out in obedience to the Lord, not knowing what the outcome would eventually be.

What I gleaned from Hagar's story is that during seasons of brokenness, you should neither run ahead of God nor run away from Him. He will come to your rescue and give you instructions on how to proceed. Don't move until you have direction from Him. Proverbs 3:5-6 says, *"Trust in the Lord with all your heart and lean not on your own understanding; in all your ways submit to him, and he will make your paths straight."*

There is Blessing in Brokenness

In the process of brokenness, we only see the chaos in our lives and wonder if things will ever get better. We feel the pain, confusion, and disorientation, and can't believe this is really happening to us. When I look back, I remember my former pastor telling me once, "God is going to break you." That seemed very harsh considering what I was going through at the time. I asked myself, "Am I really in such bad shape that God had to break me?"

You may not always understand why God allows certain things, but you can be sure God is not making any mistakes. In 2004, I went through one of the most challenging times in ministry. The Lord revealed to me that this situation would one day become part of my story.

In March of 2004, I was asked to step down from my full-time ministry position for no apparent reason at the time after years of faithful service. It was quite a blow to me. In the middle of my tears, the Spirit of the Lord instructed me to write down my personal account of faith and the challenge I was facing. It was difficult getting my mind and my heart to line up with the truth that God was doing something new in my life. My heart knew the truth, but my mind tried to take over by feeding me with negative thoughts based on my natural circumstances.

I came to understand this was a time of brokenness, not due to any wrong-doing on my part, but because the Father was preparing me for a greater purpose. A time in which I had to depend on Him solely in faith. It seemed so hard to do. My mind kept returning to all that I thought I had lost, but my heart would say, "Lord, I don't want to place anything above you." Scripture says, "*Whoever tries to keep their life will lose it, and whoever loses their life will preserve it.*" [8] By grace, I found my true life in Him and didn't want to lose it. In my brokenness, God remained faithful to me.

Closed Doors, Open Doors

So, what happened? Ministry wasn't going well. One day there was a staff meeting to discuss several ministry changes. At one point during the meeting, the ministry overseer asked a few of the staff members if they would miss me when I was gone. It was a setup! Each one said "no." Wow, if there was ever a time I had to exercise self-control, it was then. Can you imagine people whom you've spent years of your life with saying they wouldn't miss you if you left?

Next, I was given an official termination notice and told I had to clean out and turn in my ministry vehicle. In most cases the boss would just ask you to clean out your desk before you depart. I stuttered as I asked, "What's up with the car?" I was told that I had to turn it in because the car had an unpaid balance. If I could afford to pay for it, I could keep the car. I was heartbroken. My mind said, "Not my car, that's not fair. Is this all I get after ten years of service? Really? God, where are you in all of this?"

Several of my fellow ministers had departed the ministry earlier, angry at the "man of God." I did not want to be angry. As I was preparing to leave, he said to me, "I believe I still have your blessing in my mouth. I advise you to come to church." My mind was thinking, "Yeah right!"

Now, many of you may be thinking, that makes no sense. And it didn't at the time. At one point, I expressed my need to find a job to support myself and my children. The pastor replied, "You're so hardheaded." I felt like a child getting reprimanded.

When I spoke with the "woman of God," she said I needed to pray. That was usually her answer whenever I shared some concern with her. She is a prayer warrior. I recall the first time she encouraged me to pray during a difficult circumstance involving my marriage. I thought she would pray with me after counseling me. Instead, she encouraged me to pray for myself. I admire her for this because it helped me learn to go to God in prayer for my needs.

She also said she could not understand what I was saying, because she was of the faith. My mind was really talking to me that day. I thought if I wasn't struggling with my faith, maybe this would not be happening to me. Of course, that wasn't true. Later, I called her to apologize and follow the instructions I had been given. I made a sincere effort to regroup as quickly as possible. I needed to act in faith. I didn't want to give any more place to the devil.

The next day I spent quietly in my room desperate to hear from God. In an attempt to pull myself together, I started reading a chapter from one of Charles Swindoll's books, "*The Mystery of God's Will*" because His will in all of this was definitely a mystery.

I marvel at how God is faithful to give us the very word we need in times of difficulty. In the chapter, "*Closed Doors, Open Doors*," Swindoll says, "Most of life is learning and growing, falling and getting back up, forgiving and forgetting, accepting and going on." [9] He explained that God is like a potter, and we are the clay. At times, the potter will suddenly mash the clay down and start over again. Been there, felt that. He also said that God is "shaping us into the image of His Son, regardless of the pain and heartache that may require." [10]

Swindoll further said, "[God] alone has the right to open a door of opportunity and escort us through it. As He walks with us, we persevere through the doors He opens. He also has the right to slam doors without explanation. More often than not, when a door of opportunity is shut, it is to lead us through a better door with greater opportunities."[11] I thought to myself, if a new door is open, you'd better not look back, or else the door may close on you. Such a great revelation. I should have seen that months ago.

Another eye-opener for me was, "Anytime you try to force a door, thinking you'll get your way, ultimately you will regret it. Leave it closed, back away, accept it. With acceptance is peace."[12] I felt I had a part of the answer, so I decided to accept what happened and go on. It took faith to accept this change. My mind was still struggling with thoughts of what happened. Sometimes, in closing doors, God is teaching us an invaluable lesson—to trust Him in all of your circumstances, whether good or bad.

Many times, we have no idea what ministry leaders go through while waiting for the manifestation of God's promise. One misconception about salvation and Christianity is that it takes away all pain, and solves every problem. Some think that if a Christian suffers hardship, it is because there is unresolved sin in that person's life. However, this is not what this experience has taught me. It taught me that we will experience suffering. Christianity is about endurance and perseverance of faith as we walk along our path.

Since that time, I have experienced many open and closed doors. I've learned that God is sovereign and in full control. I don't have to carry the burden. It's up to God to make the plan work. My role is to walk in obedience to His will, regardless of the circumstances. I trusted the Lord through this by not pushing my way in the direction I thought I was supposed to go, and God opened new doors. I realized that it was necessary to close the previous door for me to walk through the new one.

Because of obeying God, doing His will, accepting the closed doors, and walking through the open ones, my perspective changed. I was no longer looking from my limited viewpoint, but seeing from God's perspective.

Maybe you've come to a closed door, and you've been pushing it, trying to get it to open again. You've looked for someone to blame, and it's hard for you to accept the fact that the door is truly closed. I encourage you to accept it, give up the fight, let it be, and allow God to bring you through the doors He opens for you. Don't miss what God has for you on the other side of the closed door.

What I also learned is that God was maturing me spiritually, taking me from the place I was to the place He wanted me to be. Throughout my journey this has been the process He has used to develop, change, and mature my faith. In all of this, I needed to learn to embrace what He was allowing in my life to equip me for the future. He may not deal with you in the same way He dealt with me, but if He does, perhaps this will help you see His hand in it quicker than I did.

God Orders Your Footsteps

God uses various trials and tests to refine you and purge off the dross or impurities in your life. According to *Easton's Bible Dictionary*, dross is the impurities of silver separated from the one in the process of melting.[13] Proverbs 25:4 says, "*Remove the dross from the silver, and a silversmith can produce a vessel.*"

There will be tests of your faith, obedience, availability, commitment, values, contentment, and vision for what God is doing in your life. He desires for you to trust Him no matter how things look. You must accept your testing with joy. Job said, "*He knows the way I should take; when He has tested me, I will come forth as gold.*"[14]

You must arise in the Spirit in obedience to move forward in the will of

God. When you retain the option to turn back, you lose your spiritual edge. You lose the power of your faith. If we don't make room to sharpen our spiritual lives, we become dull. It's difficult to maintain the spiritual energy, focus, and drive necessary to follow Christ when you are going through hard times, but He will preserve you and keep your foot from slipping, and bring you into a place of abundance when you praise Him in your circumstances. Psalm 66:8-12 says to praise Him because "*He has preserved our lives and kept our feet from slipping. . . we went through fire and water, but you brought us to a place of abundance.*"

God sets you on the right path, and it is up to you to follow it. He tests, refines, and brings us to a place of abundance. Trust that He will make good what He has spoken to you. During this difficult season, the Lord shared with me that this was the path He ordained for me to take to reach the abundant life in Him—the path of restoration, faith, and holiness to reach my destiny, leaving behind every weight that would hinder me from carrying His glory.

> "*Dear friends, do not be surprised at the fiery ordeal that has come on you to test you, as though something strange were happening to you. But rejoice inasmuch as you participate in the sufferings of Christ, so that you may be overjoyed when his glory is revealed.*"[15]

Seeing from God's perspective

> "*Very truly I tell you, unless a kernel of wheat falls to the ground and dies, it remains only a single seed. But if it dies, it produces many seeds.*" – *John 12:24*

Does God care? I'm sure Hagar felt invisible to God and to the people in her life. Yes, people noticed her, but did they really see her? Did God really see her? Did they see the young woman who obediently served her master, only to find herself homeless?

The process of brokenness goes against what we are taught in today's culture. How can we serve a God who allows us to go through so much pain? What I've learned is that He will lead you through great affliction, pain, and distress that you may feel you are unable to bear. Yet, it is during these times of brokenness we learn to rely on Him. "*Trust in the Lord with all your heart and lean not on your own understanding; in all your ways submit to him, and he will make your paths straight.*"[16]

God only wants the best for us. As young girls, we all may have had dreams of marriage, buying a home with the white picket fence, going on family vacations, and happy holiday gatherings—good jobs, wonderful kids, and a nice home. This is the so-called American Dream. And for many, that dream has been shattered. You never, ever, ever dreamed you'd be without your spouse because they died prematurely. For others, you just thought divorce was a word that could never touch you. You never thought your son or daughter would become addicted to drugs or have a child out of wedlock. Nor did you think you would lose your home at a time when the economy faltered. So, what do you do when your world seems to be falling apart?

When Your World Falls Apart

The Hebrew name Hagar means "one who flees" or "one who seeks refuge." The story of Hagar and her son, Ishmael, is the story of millions of exploited, trafficked, disabled, and rejected women and children, and just like Hagar, God hears their cries.

I can imagine what happened left Hagar reeling from the pain of rejection. Here is a young woman who, in obedience to her mistress, sleeps with her mistress' husband. She is left with a young child and evicted from the place she considers home with no means of taking care of herself or her child.

Fourteen years after Hagar's return to Abraham's household, Sarah bears her own son. Again, due to jealousy, she forces Hagar and Ishmael to leave. They return to the desert and wander there without hope. Finally, when their water runs out, she places her son under a bush and walks away to weep at a distance, as she could not bear to watch him die. God again hears their cries. An angel of God calls to Hagar and says, *"Do not be afraid; God has heard the boy crying."*[17] The angel of God reminds Hagar of God's blessing and provides a spring of water for them. They survive and prosper, and Ishmael becomes a great nation as God had promised.

In these days, it is critical for us to see things from God's perspective and not man's. As human beings, we tend to see things in the natural, while God sees things in the supernatural. We see what is in front of us, while He sees the beginning, the now and the end. Without this heavenly perspective, the impact of our prayers could be limited because we will craft them from within the narrow scope of an earthbound view of reality. He wants us to see the unseen and understand spiritual things.[18]

Maybe you are facing a time of brokenness, and it feels as though the emotional pain is more than you can bear. Or perhaps you are dealing with a series of disappointments that have completely undermined your sense of security. Instead of becoming fearful, ask the Lord to reveal what He is teaching you.

Paul encouraged us to keep a heavenly perspective. He based his instruction on some basic truths. When we begin to grasp these truths, and make them part of our everyday thinking patterns, our minds will begin to have a heavenly focus.

> *"Therefore, if you have been raised with Christ, keep seeking the things above, where Christ is, seated at the right hand of God. Keep thinking about things above, not things on the earth, for you have died and your life is hidden with Christ in God. When*

Christ (who is your life) appears, then you too will be revealed in glory with him."[19]

If we are going to partner with God to bring Heaven to Earth, we must first learn to see from Heaven's viewpoint. *"For My thoughts are not your thoughts, nor are your ways My ways," says the Lord. "For as the heavens are higher than the earth, so are My ways higher than your ways, and My thoughts than your thoughts."*[20]

The pain of brokenness can be a deep hurt. My heart was crushed as if it had been stomped on, broken, and discarded. Unable to progress in my work or relationships, I was becoming a hostage to my own sadness.

Brokenness enables us to experience God's grace. The Lord taught the apostle that His grace would always be sufficient for all of Paul's weaknesses. Your weakness is an opportunity for God to show His power in your life. Time and time again during seasons of great struggle, I experienced God grace and power to overcome my weaknesses.

You can have confidence, knowing that God hears your cry and has already orchestrated the things that concern you. You don't have to worry over your circumstances. Just remain steadfast and unmovable, being confident that, *"He who began a good work in you will carry it on to completion until the day of Christ Jesus."*[21] Every aspect of your life is in His hands.

Brokenness is a blessing, but too often we're so caught up with wanting to feel better or wanting things to happen immediately that we miss God's best for us. No one enjoys the pain of brokenness. God balances our lives by giving us enough blessings to keep us happy and enough burdens to keep us humble. Ecclesiastes 7:14 says, *"When times are good, be happy; but when times are bad, consider this: God has made the one as well as the other."* Like Hagar, we are called to respond to God's divine grace in faithful obedience, despite the godless culture in which we live.

Are you willing?

Failing Forward

"The difference between average people and achieving people is their perception of and response to failure." – John C. Maxwell[22]

No one likes to fail, yet God uses failure to prepare us for future success, to get our lives back on track, and to help us see more clearly. Another fruit of failure is the ability to understand the sorrows of others. It helps us see others more compassionately.

Failure brings pain, and it can drive us to Him or, if not dealt with properly, away from Him. Fear of failure can stop you from moving forward in God. It can also cause you to procrastinate – stealing your time, energy, and potential. During a season in which I thought I failed, I learned that is important to neither run ahead of God nor run away from Him. I needed to trust that He would come to my rescue and give me new instructions on how to move forward.

Mary the Mother of Jesus

I don't think I can talk about obedience without talking about Mary, the mother of Jesus. She is a woman admired for her bravery and loved for her devotion to God. She walked a difficult path, knowing how costly her submission would be.

Mary was highly favored of God and chosen to be the mother of Jesus Christ. We know the angel Gabriel visits Mary to bring her the news of God's plan. When the angel Gabriel tells Mary that she will become pregnant and give birth to the Son of God, she asks him how that would even be possible because she was a virgin and not yet married. Then the angel responds to her and said: *"For no word from God will ever fail."*[23]

A . FRANCINE GREEN

Though she is young and most likely poor, Mary has something priceless inside—she is a woman of faith who loves God deeply. She is a willing servant who trusts God and obeys His call, having an obedient spirit. Mary's service to God does not end when Jesus was born. She mothers Jesus for thirty years as He grows into manhood. At the time of Jesus Christ's crucifixion, she is among the group of disciples who follow Him. I can't imagine what she was thinking as she watched her son die in such an excruciating manner. Mary was a woman truly blessed by God, chosen to be a part of His plan of redemption of mankind.

ENDNOTES

1 Samuel 15:22-23

Job 36:11 (MEV)

Stanley, Charles F, "*The Blessings of Brokenness: Why God Allows Us to Go Through Hard Times,*" (Grand Rapids, MI: Zondervan Publishing House, 1997).

Fletcher, Elizabeth, Hagar – Bible Woman, *Women of the Bible*, Web. July 6, 2017, www.womeninthebible.net

Genesis 16:7-13

Ibid.

Ibid.

Luke 17:33

Swindoll, Charles R, "*The Mystery of God's Will, What Does He Want from Me?*" (Dallas, TX: Word Pub, 1999), March 25, 2017. 184.

Swindoll, 187.

Swindoll, 188.

Ibid.

"Dross," *BibleStudyTools.com,* Easton's Bible Dictionary, Web. March 25, 2017, http://www.biblestudytools.com/search/?s=references&q=dross.

Job 23:40

1 Peter 4:12

Proverbs 3:5-6

Genesis 21:17:18

2 Corinthians 4:18

Colossians 3:1-4

Isaiah 55:8

Philippians 1:6

Maxwell, John, "*Failing Forward – Turning Mistakes into Stepping Stones for Success,*" (Nashville, TN: Thomas Nelson, 2007). 2.

Luke 1:37

Chapter 7

THE "ESHET CHAYIL" WOMAN

"Have I not commanded you? Be strong and courageous. Do not
be afraid; do not be discouraged, for the Lord your God will be
with you wherever you go."
Joshua 1:9

The call to follow, obey, and trust God involves strength and courage. There have been many great men and women of faith who have gone before us, accomplishing what seemed impossible, and blazing a trail for us to follow. Joshua is one of the Bible's greatest military leaders. He is best known as Moses' second in command who takes over and leads the Israelites into the Promised Land after Moses' death. Joshua's boldness, courage, and determination to obey God encourages me to be strong and courageous as I pursue God's purpose. Whenever I become discouraged or face new challenges, I meditate on Joshua 1:9. Courage is defined as mental or moral strength to venture, persevere, and withstand danger, fear, or difficulty.[1] It required great courage and strength when Joshua took over the leadership of Israel after Moses has died. Over and over again, the Lord told Joshua to "*be strong and courageous.*"

Being courageous doesn't mean you will never be afraid. It means press into God for the strength and courage you need to overcome fear with faith. Sometimes your mind may even start racing away with all kinds of "what if" thoughts. But when this happens, you should kick into overdrive and let the Word of God take over. You have to trust God beyond your fears, knowing that He has already worked things out on your behalf. Isaiah 41:10 says, "*Do not fear, for I am with you; do not be dismayed, for I am your God. I will strengthen you and help you; I will uphold you with my righteous right hand.*"

Woman of Valor

When you read Proverbs 31, you may wonder, "Who is this woman? How can she possibly manage to do all of this and survive?" This woman seems to have it all together. No doubt, many women have felt unable to live up to her faultless example of womanhood. I know I have. Yet, there is much we can learn from the virtuous woman.

For starters, Proverbs 31 is a poem of praise to an excellent wife. It is a Jewish tradition to read or sing at the beginning of Shabbat, on Friday night at the dinner table. Husbands sing this celebration of womanhood to their wives to honor them for making the house a home. Proverbs 31: 29–31 says, "*Many women do noble things, but you surpass them all. Charm is deceptive, and beauty is fleeting; but a woman who fears the Lord is to be praised. Honor her for all that her hands have done, and let her works bring her praise at the city gate.*" No doubt, many women do not think of blessing, honor, or praise when they hear Proverbs 31:10-31. They read her accomplishments and feel like they can never live up to the standard this woman embodies.

> "*Who Can Find an Eshet Chayil Woman? She is worth far more than rubies.*" – *Proverbs 31:10*

How does the Proverbs 31 woman relate to having courage? Let's unpack this a little more and take a closer look at this awesome woman. Proverbs 31 isn't about being superwoman. It's not about being perfect. It is a poem in praise of women. It is about bravery, courage, and strength. Her example reveals the potential within each one of us which, if properly understood, will transform our personal lives and the world around us as we carry out the many roles within our sphere of influence as women.

She is a heroine and role model for what we should all aspire to. She embodies the qualities of insight, patience, influence, and balance. I like to think of her as *"poetry in motion."* She is someone who moves with tactful elegance, with graceful confidence and courage to accomplish all she sets her heart to do.

The Hebrew word *eshet* is a construct from *isha* (woman), and *chayil* (bravery; capability; triumph; a rampart; or wealth).[2] The *eshet chayil* then represents virtues of courage and strength. *Eshet Chayil* is a woman who has risen above the others. She is not only strong and courageous, but she is business-savvy. She is a competent leader and force for God. To know her is to appreciate her strength, insight, talents and grace. She uses her wisdom, faithfulness and obedience to God to accomplish all that she has been given to do.

We all need courage to face the everyday challenges of life, big and small; to confront our own inner conflicts and to choose faith, hope and love over despair and skepticism. We need courage to love our enemies and bless those who persecute us; to stand for Christ in a culture which opposes and ridicules our faith; and to hear God's calling on our lives and pursue it, however difficult it may be.

A woman can bring glory to God with her life whether she is married or single, a mother or childless. Ruth is such a woman. She is a truly remarkable person of character. In Ruth 1-2, we see that even in the face of tremendous loss, she is loyal to her mother-in-law, vowing to follow her wherever she goes and provide for her once they arrive. Ruth is a woman of valor because she lived her life with incredible bravery, wisdom, and strength. She is a fierce woman because she puts her trust in an Almighty God. She is you, every time you trust in God and do not lean on your own understanding, every time you ask for wisdom, and every time you obey God despite the circumstances you face.

Women Who Exhibited Great Courage

Have you ever had anyone make you a promise? You waited and waited and waited for the promise to manifest although it appears it would never come to pass. You become frustrated and are tempted to give up, thinking maybe you misinterpreted what you heard. Maybe you try to make it happen yourself. If you are having doubts and insecurities about God's promises, you are not alone.

I am inspired by women who defy incredible obstacles to accomplish God's purposes. This is a story of five courageous sisters who were willing to lay it all on the line to possess what was rightfully theirs. These amazing women showed outstanding courage in the face of difficult circumstances.

In Numbers 27, after the forty years in the wilderness, and toward the end of Moses' life, there is a fascinating story of five sisters: Mahlah, Noah, Hoglah, Milcah, and Tirzah, the daughters of a man named Zelophehad. The story begins in Egypt with God's people struggling under tyranny and injustice. When Zelophehad dies, his teenage daughters face a tough decision: do they accept the status quo of a male-dominated society, or risk everything and claim their father's inheritance?

Zelophehad is a faithful man of character and principle. This man is of the tribe of Manasseh and unfortunately dies during the wilderness journey. He has five daughters, but no sons. In Numbers 26, a census is taken of all males over the age of twenty. As the census is concluded, God instructs Moses to apportion the land as shares among all the males. Zelophehad's daughters are not counted in the census and are not to receive any land as an inheritance. However, the present interpretation of the law is inequitable because it excludes women who have no brother, father, or husband.

Because Zelophehad has no sons, his daughters are exempt from the portion of the land to which he was entitled. When he dies in the journey to Canaan, his daughters realize they are going to be left out of the promise. They have to develop a strategy. Although they are determined to claim their rights, these women keep their mouths closed until the right time. They don't spend their time whining and complaining about how unfair the law is towards women.

Let's imagine the scene: the Israelite camp is formed of tribes, each of whom has a determined place, with the tabernacle in the middle. In the center stand the main authority figures, who are all men: Moses, the priest Eleazar, and the chiefs. Imposing as this structure may have been, these five sisters decide to claim their rights.

These young women approach Moses and the rulers of the people to ask if the land that would have been given to their father might be given to them instead. Up to that time, no provision was made in the law for property or possessions to be passed down to women when there are no living male sons. All five sisters are standing before the entire counsel at the doorway of the tabernacle of meeting. Now, just imagine these teenage girls "pulling up" on Moses and the leaders, telling them they want their father's inheritance. Visualize the scene of these sisters coming forward publicly before the assembly of leaders, officials, and the entire community to present their case. These women truly exemplify faith, courage, humility, temperance, and patience.

In Numbers 27, they begin their appeal by reminding Moses of their father's integrity and reputation. Because this is an unusual situation, Moses has to take the matter to God for directions on how to handle it. God tells Moses the women are right and that the property should be given to them as an inheritance among their father's relatives. God's answer is an excellent example of His fairness to both men and women and how laws can be changed.

Most of us, like Zelophehad's daughters, were once without hope of an inheritance – "*strangers from the covenants of promise, having no hope, and without God in the world.*"[3] We became heirs of the promise when we accepted Jesus Christ as our Lord and Savior by faith. Like these earnest women, we now eagerly desire our part.

Are you willing to go the distance to possess your God-given inheritance? If you want to leave your desert and embrace all God has promised, you can allow the daughters of Zelophehad to show you the way. James 4:2 says, "*You do not have because you do not ask God.*" These five sisters were not afraid to ask for their inheritance.

ENDNOTES

1. *"Courage," Merriam-Webster.com*, Merriam-Webster, Web. 8 Apr. 2017.
2. Parsons, John J.,"*Eshet Chayil – Praising a Woman of Valor – Hebrews for Christians,*" Hebrews For Christians, April 8, 2017, http://www.hebrew4christians.com/Blessings/Shabbat_Blessings/Eshet_Chayil/eshet_chayil.html.
3. Ephesians 2:12

Chapter 8

MY TIMES ARE IN YOUR HANDS

"My times are in your hands."
Psalm 31:15

It is important that we understand the timing and seasons God has ordained for our lives. Ecclesiastes 3:1 tells us, *"There is a time for everything, and a season for every activity under the heavens."* The Hebrew word for "seasons" is *moed,* which literally translated means "appointed times" or "divine appointments."[1]

God determines the timing of the things that should take place in your life. I had to understand that God's timing is not always my timing. Often, we want things to happen in a hurry, but God doesn't work that way. When I began to grasp an understanding of times and seasons, I realized that my times were in His hands. I began to understand that His timing will always be perfect. Psalm 18:30 says, His *"way is perfect."*

His timing is never late, and it is never early. Understanding this kept me from running ahead of God and trying to make things happen on my own.

Most of us tend to worry when it looks as though things are delayed. We get stressed out because we want what we want and would prefer it right now. God knows the desires of our hearts, and He knows better than we do what is necessary or good for us.

Waiting on God isn't always easy. He will not move until you both are ready. Keys to understanding God's timing involve patience and trust. Our patience or lack thereof often reveals our trust in His timing. Learn to be patient as you wait expectantly for Him to do something great in your life. Patience is how you act while you are waiting on God to do what only He can do. It's an attitude that has been forged through the fire of affliction.

We see this clearly when the Lord instructs Moses to go tell Pharaoh, "*Let my people go, so that they may worship me.*"[2] (Exodus 9:1). When Pharaoh refuses, the Lord sends a plague: "*The LORD set a time and said, "Tomorrow the LORD will do this in the land.*"[3]

When you pursue God's plan for your life, you will run into delays. God uses those times of waiting to prepare you and test you so that you will be able to face whatever is coming in the next phase of your journey. I recall the Holy Spirt saying to me during a season of transition, "Keep in mind, you do not want something you can feel and touch at the expense of rejecting what I have already ordained for you." The Lord told me this during a season in which I was anxious, feeling inadequate and useless. My heart longed to serve, yet I felt like I had been benched from participating in what He was doing. You can trust God's timing. In seasons of transition we learn to be still before the Lord and wait patiently for him.

I recall the Lord speaking to me once through a prophetic word:

> *"Trust Me when you feel that the process is too difficult. Know that it is I who works in you both to will and to do for My good pleasure. Do not say that this is an uncomfortable place, but know that it is necessary to bring you into My purpose and plan for your life."*

I was uncomfortable and pushed pass my feelings, learning to trust and obey His Word during these times.

Seasons of Transition

At the end of 2016, I sensed the Holy Spirit leading me to step down from my ministry position at the church I was serving in preparation for the next level of ministry. This was a very painful transition, not because of the ministry position, but because it meant letting go of the familiar which can be extremely difficult to depart from. There are usually lots of mixed emotions and wondering if you are truly hearing from God.

I'm a sentimental person who sometimes get attached to people and places. Yet I found grace for this transition because I knew I was following the Holy Spirit's leading. What I have learned over the years is that when God is directing you to make a change, He will confirm it by two or three witnesses. It may not come as a verbal confirmation, yet He may reveal it through others who are either sensing or experiencing the same thing.

The final confirmation came when I sensed the Holy Spirit saying, "You have to leave the familiar place completely"—meaning I couldn't have one foot in and the other foot out. I had to be all in or all out. Why? Spiritual blessings often are not realized until you move fully in the direction God shows you.

Abraham, the father of faith, began his spiritual journey when the Lord said:

"Go for yourself [for your own advantage] away from your country, from your relatives and your father's house, to the land I will show you. And I will make of you a great nation, and I will bless you [with abundant increase of favors] and make your name famous and distinguished, and you will be a blessing [dispensing good to others]."[4]

It may be difficult to comprehend why God was asking Abraham to do this. God told him to leave his native country, his relatives, and his father's family. Why would God ask him to do such a thing? Family is important, right? I can imagine God saying to Abraham, "Leave everything behind that you know to be familiar. Everything that feels comfortable. Everything that feels like home, and follow me to a new place." To top it off, Abraham was told to leave everything behind with no idea where God was asking him to go.

God didn't give Abraham a detailed map or even show him the destination. What He did tell Abraham is that He would bless him and his descendants if Abraham obeyed him. "So, Abraham departed and did as the Lord instructed" (Genesis 12:4). Abraham may not have had many details on where God was taking him, but by faith, Abraham trusted that there were things God had for him in this new, unfamiliar place.

So, I stepped out, just as Abraham, and did what the Lord directed. The Lord later revealed to me that I had become too comfortable and had to choose between the ministry position or moving forward in faith to fulfill His purposes. I could experience the fullness of God's plan for me or remain in a comfortable position. Don't forfeit the promises of God because you are too busy being comfortable in the familiar.

During seasons of transition, it is important to trust in the Lord. There will be things that you may not understand with your natural mind, but move forward in faith and obedience in what the Lord is asking you to do. I realize this new level of ministry He has called me to marks a new season in my life, one where I will be taken out of my comfort zone and into many of the things God revealed to me during my season of preparation. I began to see the manifestation of promises made long ago. I didn't know exactly where God was taking me next but I trusted that it would be a good place—a place of blessing. I know in my heart of hearts that God will continue to direct my path as I walk in obedience to His will.

We must be able to interpret times and seasons of change. Some things God will only give us when we step outside of our "familiar" places.

Shifting into a New Season

"You go before me and follow me. You place your hand of blessing on my head." – Psalm 139:5

When shifting into a new season there are some important things to remember:

1. **God goes before us**. Our heavenly Father goes before us and walks behind us too, and places His hand of blessing on us. God knows which way we are going and is there to protect us even when we can't see Him. He knows what's ahead of us. He will go before you and clear out the obstacles and make your path straight when you submit to His will.

And the same God who knows all about the time ahead promises to go with you every step of the way. He is true to His Word. He is *"with you and will watch over you wherever you go,"* and He *"will not leave you"* until He has done what He has promised you.[5] God himself will be your guide, and He will lead you through. He knows the challenges that you'll face and the obstacles that are before you, and

He will clear the path. Isaiah 26:7 says, "*The path of the righteous is level; you, the Upright One, make the way of the righteous smooth.*"

Whatever you face today, God has already gone before you and will guard you from behind. I encourage you to contend for the faith. "*I felt compelled to write and urge you to contend for the faith that was once for all entrusted to God's holy people.*"[6]

2. You must let go of the old to make room for the new.
"*Forget the former things; do not dwell on the past. See, I am doing a new thing! Now it springs up; do you not perceive it? I am making a way in the wilderness and streams in the wasteland.*"[7] When shifting seasons, things change in our lives that will affect our focus, vision, activities, and even our relationships. The most challenging part of shifting into a new season is letting go of things from our past season. This is where I believe most people get stuck. We tend to gravitate towards what we know, thinking the old is good, even though God has something better planned for us.

When I was directed by the Holy Spirit to come out of my comfort zone to prepare for my next season of ministry, the old season had come to an end. It was a difficult transition because it meant stepping down from a ministry position and leaving people that I dearly love. However, the choice was clear. I wanted to make the shift to prepare for the greater.

There was some fear of the unknown, but if I had not taken the leap, I would have missed how God was moving in my life. I would have missed the opportunities to grow and gain revelation through my new experiences. Our obedience to God affects not only us, but others around us. Our obedience might be the key to someone else's miracle or breakthrough. The true test of our faith and trust comes in our obedience to God.

During seasons of transition, God refines us, tests us, and purifies us so that we will be fit to carry out His purposes in the earth. No one can take your place and do what He has intended for you. During the refining process, it can get a little intense, yet He is with us in the furnace of affliction.

3. **Understand that stepping into a new season brings changes along with challenges**. Change is inevitable. It's going to happen. But God gives us revelation and truth to propel us into new and different seasons. The Bible is full of illustrations where God orchestrated some incredible circumstances to take His people where they'd never been before. He may create situations to help us to grow and go beyond where we are at in our walk with Him. Consider the story of Peter walking on water. Peter had to step out of the boat first.

Sometimes we can even experience a pause between seasons, which can be even more stressful. Wherever you are at, I want to encourage you to step out of the boat, get out of your comfort zone, and do something you have never done before.

Forgetting the Past and What's Behind You

Don't look back, look forward to where you are going. Abram was given a commission by God to leave his country, his people, and his father's household to go to the land that God would show Him. In Genesis 13:14-15, once Abram had separated from Lot, God instructs him to look up, toward the east, west, north, and south, and see the land that He would give to him and his descendants. Abraham needs to look upward to keep moving forward towards the Promised Land.

Psalm 121:1 says, "*I lift up my eyes to the mountains—where does my help come from?*" When we lift our eyes towards the Heavens, our perspective changes. In times of trouble, train yourself to look up toward the heavens, and your whole perspective will change.

One summer, while serving in ministry, our church had a gathering down on some property near the Potomac River in Maryland. My role was to help make sure the event went smoothly. When I finally took a break, I walked down to the pier and looked out onto the water. While standing there, I heard the Lord say, "Go forward and never look back." I thought the Spirit was referring to my failing marriage, but today I understand He was speaking about going forward toward my destiny and never looking back at the past.

Keep Going and Don't Look Back

As I began to transition into this new season, I heard the Lord say two things, "You can never go forward looking back!" and "You can't make progress looking backwards." If we know progress is good for us, why is it so difficult to let go? In Genesis 19, we read a noteworthy story of Abraham's nephew, Lot and his family and their time in Sodom and Gomorrah. God was preparing to destroy these two cities because all the people of Sodom were very wicked, but the Lord gives Lot and his family the opportunity to flee the city or stay behind and be destroyed, those are his options.

Angels commanded them to flee from the doomed city Sodom. They warned the group not to look back. The angels even took their hand to hurry them on their way, but Lot and his wife lingered, reluctant to leave their home.

"When he hesitated, the men grasped his hand and the hands of his wife and of his two daughters and led them safely out of the city, for the Lord was merciful to them." As soon as they had brought them out, one of them said, *"Flee for your lives! Don't look back, and don't stop anywhere in the plain! Flee to the mountains or you will be swept away!"*[8]

Lot's wife was the only one who disobeyed the angel's warning and looked back at the destruction of the doomed city. As a result, she *"became a pillar of salt."*[9] I don't know what caused Lot's wife to look back; perhaps it was her ties to the city. All we can do is learn from her mistake. Jesus warns us today that it will be just like this on the day the Son of Man is revealed. He says, *"Remember Lot's wife."*[10]

Remember how Ruth and Naomi kept going while never looking back and experienced the blessings of God? Ruth loves her mother-in-law Naomi, and has great compassion for her, because of the tremendous loss of not only her husband, but both of her sons. Ruth's sister-in-law, Orpah, makes the choice to go back to her people in Moab, but Ruth cannot bear to part from Naomi or from the God of Israel that she had come to know. When you have an option to go back, you forfeit the plan of God for your life. You must have perseverance, and resolute tenacity when pursuing your destiny.

Ruth told Naomi:

"Don't urge me to leave you or to turn back from you. Where you go I will go, and where you stay I will stay. Your people will be my people and your God my God. Where you die I will die, and there I will be buried. May the Lord deal with me, be it ever so severely, if even death separates you and me."[11]

Ruth has an open mind and a teachable spirit, so she listens to Naomi and takes her advice in relationship to Boaz. Ruth follows Naomi's instructions to the letter, trusts the Lord, and He rewards her faithfulness.

If Ruth had looked back to what was lost, she would not have had the opportunity to marry Boaz. Her loyalty certainly resulted in long-term good. In an unexpected way, God allows Ruth to remarry and give birth to a son named Obed, who becomes grandfather to King David.

To move forward, we must forget things that are behind us and reach forward to things ahead of us. Forgetting those things which are behind is perhaps one of the greatest challenges we may face, especially when those "things" were a major part of our daily lives. I've had to forget past failures, disappointments, financial loss, and more to move forward into God's purposes. Sometimes moving on feels like leaving a piece of yourself behind. When you are in between phases, you may feel there is a tug of war in your soul attempting to tear you apart. I assure you, you can move ahead and press on toward the goal with joy.

The Power of Your Life's Message

I never considered that my life would be or have a message. But as I pressed into God through prayer and praise, and spent time meditating on His Word, I discovered my life's message. This practice caused me to be sensitive and obedient to the Holy Spirit's leading. Had I not found my life's message and purpose, I may have not had the opportunity to speak into the lives of those needing insight from someone who's been there. The Bible encourages believers to comfort and encourage others just as God comforted us in our troubles so that we can comfort others.

Imagine the people needing your insight having to live a long time without it because of your delay? Ouch. That's a hard but real truth. There are countless people in need of spiritual advisors, counselors and a timely word in season that will shift their lives in the direction God has ordained. "*Plans fail for lack of counsel, but with many advisers they succeed. A person finds joy in giving an apt reply—and how good is a timely word.*"[12]

God uses ordinary, everyday circumstances to help you become the person He created you to be now and for eternity. The road you choose to travel along this journey shapes your character, personality, and passion for life. Our life's message can be heard in what we say, seen in how we live, and it is reflected in the choices we make.

My journey has shaped what I have become and continues to conform me into the image of Christ as I continue to pursue Him. *"For those God foreknew he also predestined to be conformed to the image of his Son, that he might be the firstborn among many brothers and sisters."*[13]

I've learned that one cannot have a mindset or preconceived notion about how God does things. God works everything out in agreement with the counsel and design of His own will. You must have a sincere desire to know God more to fulfill your purpose and embrace God's calling on your life. As I moved forward, the Holy Spirit was leading, guiding, and equipping me.

To reach your destiny, you must take the path of holiness, faith, and restoration to walk in the abundant life Christ paid the price for you to have. You can't take the old baggage with you because the spiritual gate is narrow. Don't go back to the old familiar things when times get hard. Each level comes with a test of your obedience, so move forward from faith to faith.

Grace furnishes what is lacking in our lives. Not merely what we want, but what we need to sustain us in life. Things come to you when you follow the path God ordained. You don't have to chase after them. I remember the Lord asking me once, *"Will you trust me even if it looks like you are being deceived?"* It wasn't that I was being deceived. It was a test of my faith to trust Him not matter what things looked like in the natural.

There will be a supernatural shift as God takes you from one level to the next level. God will transition you from one place to another or one position to another as you grow in faith and obedience to His will. He will position you to step into a new level of authority in the Spirit to accomplish His plans.

My daily confession became: "I am shifting into a new place with God. Jesus is leading me into a new place." Pray for God to renew your vision, rekindle your spirit especially during challenging times, and restore your passion for Him. Pray to wake up each day and take if by force.

It's normal to feel inadequate when you are pursuing your God-given purpose. But can any good come from it? Yes, remember Christ fills our inadequacy. When our weaknesses drive us to God, He fills up what is lacking in our lives strengthening our faith as we experience His awesome power in our lives. Our confidence and competency is not in ourselves, but in Christ. "*Such confidence we have through Christ before God. Not that we are competent in ourselves to claim anything for ourselves, but our competence comes from God.*"[14]

The Making of a Prophet

I accepted salvation as a young child. At the time, I had no idea that later in life the Holy Spirit would lead me down a path that would open a whole new realm of understanding for me. A realm that was totally beyond my comprehension. I never spent time reading my Bible, so I knew nothing about Old and New Testament prophets, let alone modern-day prophets proclaiming the Word of the Lord. What's even more fascinating was when the Holy Spirit began to stir me in that direction. I now understand He was revealing a call to prophetic ministry.

I begin hearing the still, small voice of the Holy Spirit in my heart. Like a sponge, I began soaking up everything the Holy Spirit was revealing to me. Jeremiah 33:3 says, "*Call to me and I will answer you and tell you great and unsearchable things you do not know.*" My hunger and thirst for God grew more and more with each passing day.

Many tests and temptations come when you are growing in the prophetic. They are meant to mature you in your gifting and calling. Trials come in periodic intervals in our lives as well as intense seasons that sometimes feel like they will never end. Don't fear, God can turn your trials into triumph. The key to victory is to keep your eyes focused on Jesus. God's grace enabled Paul not only to accept his afflictions, but also to glory in them. God can transform your weakness into strength. Paul was suffering for the sake of Jesus Christ and glorified God by the way he accepted and handled the difficult experiences of life.

During one trial, I felt as though I wouldn't make it. The Lord said to me: "As you go through the pressure I will comfort you. In your heart, you feel like you are dying and you are so that you will learn to rely on Me. Don't despair, I will deliver you. I have not forsaken you."

Throughout this season of preparation, the Lord was developing my spiritual hearing, my ability to see with spiritual eyes, and my obedience to Him. Prior to this time, I didn't understand what it meant to see and hear in the Spirit. One of the most exciting aspects of living a prophetic lifestyle, is the way Scriptures come to life by the anointing of the Holy Spirit through divine encounters. The Lord revealed His great love and grace for mankind through my encounters with Him. Revelation is when God reveals something to you that you did not understand before. The Apostle Paul prayed for the Ephesians, asking that God "*give you the Spirit of wisdom and revelation, so that you may know Him better.*"[15]

God bought me through many dry places. It is in these places I recognized that I am nothing without Him. With each trial, our hearts become tender and pliable. Ezekiel 36:26-27 says, "*I will give you a new heart and put a new spirit in you; I will remove from you your heart of stone and give you a heart of flesh. And I will put my Spirit in you and move you to follow my decrees and be careful to keep my laws.*" With each trial, God cleanses our heart to bring healing and deliverance so that we may pursue His purposes. He is Jehovah Rapha–God the Healer. "*He said, 'If you listen carefully to the voice of the LORD your God and do what is right in his eyes, if you pay attention to his commands and keep all his decrees. . . for I am the LORD, who heals you.*'"[16]

Many things in your life will attempt to depress you, discourage you, and distract you so be determined and confident that you can make it to the other side. The Lord is with you wherever you go. You are ready to cross over into a new land. The moment you cross over, you will never have to look back. Remember, when God tells you to do something, He gives you the strength to do it because with Him, all things are possible!

Fear and discouragement are two enemies that attempt to stop you from sharing your message and possessing your future. Fear keeps you in the desert. The Lord says, "*Don't look anxiously about you, for I AM God. I will strengthen you. So do not fear, for I am with you; do not be dismayed, for I am your God. I will strengthen you and help you; I will uphold you with my righteous right hand.*"[17]

Focus your mind on where you are going, not where you are now. When you do, the peace of God comes over you. God desires to bring His people into revelation. The realm of the supernatural, where nothing is impossible, cannot be reasoned out in the mind. Revelation is imparted to you by the Spirit. Often revelation is not received because it is contrary to what you think you know. Revelation is coming to those with open minds and hearts ready to receive. You must have both to receive the blessings that will accompany the revelation that God is releasing in the earth today. You will go deeper and higher than you ever imagined possible before.

The Lord spoke to me again on July 20, 2004, during a challenging time saying:

> "Your time of testing in the fire of affliction has been to mold and shape your character. Testing brings forth endurance of character. I told you in the beginning to count it all joy when you go through various trials. I did not deliver you from them because I started a good work in you, developing your character, patience and endurance so that you will be wanting nothing. I AM producing long endurance in your character and the strength of quality that will never give up until you see My promise come to pass.
>
> My admonition [counsel, advise, gentle reproof] is to not get weary in well doing, that you do not let go until you see (with your natural eyes) the prize. You are one who has focus, a purpose, a goal, because you have never lost your vision of what I promised you even through the fire, the wind, and the waves. I will reward you because you have kept My promise, My Words to you, deep in your heart, no matter what you have gone through. You have never lost focus of your vision, no matter how much distraction has come your way. Remember when I spoke to you about the remnant. I call you one of my faithful remnant.
>
> So, go forth and receive from My hand a crown prepared just for you, an anointing full of My giftings. I bless you this day. This is the day I promised you where I will pour out greater works. You paid the price of faithfulness and I see I can trust you. You didn't follow me just for your reward, but because you loved ME. God works through those who are willing to pay the price to walk with Him."

Don't be discouraged because of what you feel. They are just feelings that constantly change and you cannot live by them. Learn not to give people free access to your feelings because that will hinder you. You must not be moved by what you feel in the natural to move freely in the supernatural.

As I said earlier, 2004 began an intense time of preparation for me. In 2004, the Spirit spoke to me "NOW I release you to the deliverance faith ministry I called you to. I have bought you through much to prepare you for such a time as this."

This journey with God has shaped what I have become and continues to shape me into the woman He created me to be. "*I gave up all that inferior stuff so I could know Christ personally, experience his resurrection power, be a partner in his suffering, and go all the way with him to death itself. If there was any way to get in on the resurrection from the dead, I wanted to do it.*"[18]

Defining Moments

We all experience life-defining moments. Some may be good, others bad, but they mold, shape, and direct our lives. A defining moment is a point in one's life that changes everything. It may be a moment of joy, sorrow, hope, or heartbreak. Defining moments don't all happen at once, but over the course of our lives, and they tend to happen when we least expect. During these moments, we're presented with opportunities to change our minds and correct our course if necessary. That's a good thing, because sometimes we make wrong decisions and take wrong turns. The decisions you make today will not just affect tomorrow, but will determine your future and impact the lives of others for eternity.

I have experienced many defining moments in life such as marriage, childbirth, divorce, loss of both parents, loss of a job, a fractured wrist after being struck by a car, crisis with a child, financial loss…etc. The most significant of all of these was deciding to follow Christ at all costs. Making this decision changed the way I perceive life and what is possible.

Throughout many of the above losses, I experienced God in a profound way. *"With man this is impossible, but with God all things are possible."*[19]

There are many promises from God in Scripture. We come into agreement with His promises when we say, "Amen." Jesus said in Revelation 1:14, that He is the Amen, the witness who is faithful and true. God does not forget His promises. The promises of God are not "yes" then "no." They're not "I don't know" or "maybe so." *"For all the promises of God find their "yes" in him. That is why it is through him that we utter our "amen" to God for his glory."*[20] We can count on God to keep His promises.

We are in a season that requires us to press in for the next move of God. As you position yourself and seek His face, expect God to shift things around in your finances, family, career, and ministry. You don't want to miss the moment.

Direct your faith toward God. He is ready to fulfill those promises. Choose to live a life of faith even though you know your faith will be tested. Let go of faith in this world's system and your ability to accomplish things on your own without God. Without faith, it is *"impossible to please God, because anyone who comes to him must believe that he exists and that he rewards those who earnestly seek him."*[21] Seize the moment to step into the unique identity God fashioned for you. In the same way God had specific assignments for the men and women of the Bible, He has a specific assignment just for you to fulfill.

Embracing Your Identity and Calling

There's something so inspiring about knowing who you are in Christ and pursuing your calling. No one else can do what He has called you to do. I could never imagine being where I am today, and God is not finished with me yet.

When I started my journey, there was a burden on my heart that I just could not shake. Daily, I would pray that God would use me in ministry. I had no understanding of divine assignments or alignments. At every juncture, I needed wise counsel on how to move forward and prepare myself for my destiny. God always bought someone into my life to encourage me in my calling.

In 1995, I served as a staff member with a local ministry in southern Maryland. During that season, I faithfully served in various capacities. That is when I first began to encounter the Lord in a magnificent way! I learned to love people with a God-kind of love the world considered unlovable. I am truly thankful for the opportunity to serve and minister to the women in the ministry as well as encourage the families and women who were a part of that ministry.

In 2004, the Holy Spirit began to prepare me for the specific purpose in which God had called me to. I had no idea He was preparing to impregnate me with a fresh vision of ministering to women even though I had no desire to be involved in women's ministry. The Holy Spirit revealed that I had been given a message to be preached in its season, and that was to become my passion.

As I sought the Lord for understanding, He began to reveal to me the prophetic call on my life through the life of Deborah in Judges 4-5. Deborah was an incredible woman of faith and vision. She knew and understood God's timing and nature to deliver God's people from oppression, and received God's strategy to bring victory to her nation. Deborah knew the timing for Barak to successfully lead the army of Israel to war, and she knew how the glory of God would be manifested through a woman. Deborah made a difference in her nation's future, and I sensed that somehow, I would, too.

The Holy Spirit began to reveal things to me that I could not fathom with my natural mind. Earlier in my walk with God, I had no understanding of the prophetic, nor that this would be a call of obedience to God. In this season, I needed to have a desire to know Him more and embrace the prophetic calling on my life.

God determines the timing of the things that should happen in your life. I had to look to Him to bring to pass the events that would lead me to my destiny. He does things in His timing, according to His will. He works everything out in agreement with the counsel and design of His own will. In my season of great testing, no one knew the overwhelming struggles I faced. The Holy Spirit encouraged me to never lose sight of the fact that the difficult events in my life often become the means by which God is able to use us in ministry to others. He uses various testing to refine us and purge out the trash. God wants us to trust Him no matter how things look to us. The sources that He chooses to use often test our submission, obedience, and faith.

Focused on the Goal

In 2016, I stepped out in faith and obedience establishing Beyond Church Walls Ministry. While church services and conferences are necessary for our spiritual growth and fellowship with other believers, we are to reach outside of the four walls of the church to win the lost. We are ambassadors of Christ. God is making his appeal through us. I believe others need to see a demonstration of God's power in the earth. Romans 8:19 reminds us creation is waiting eagerly for the revealing of God's sons and daughters.

When I started the ministry, I asked the Lord to reveal to me someone who was doing something similar to what He had called me to. The Spirit revealed to me through a video teaching on Deborah taught by Patricia King, which directed me to Women in Ministry Network (WIMN). WIMN is a global network of women who labor for the Lord in every sphere of influence—marketplace/business, government, media, arts and entertainment, education, the family, and the church.

WIMN connects women. It celebrates, offers apostolic encouragement, and empowers them to fulfill their God-given mandate and mission. The network is overseen by Dr. Patricia King, along with a seasoned team of advisors representing numerous fields of ministry. I felt God's leading to join the network in May 2016 knowing it was a divine arrangement. Since that time, I've also become ordained as a minister through WIMN.

What a difference saying "yes" to God can make in one's life! Saying "yes" requires total surrender of our hearts to Him. We allow God to rule in every area of our lives. When we say "yes," we can relax knowing that God is in control, and He always wants what's best for us. God has promised to lead us, teach us, and lovingly guide us—we can trust Him. When God calls, He also equips—He won't leave us to figure things out on our own.

God will not call you to be something you cannot be. The key is obedience. Obedience is a way of life that takes courage. He promises to be with you wherever you go.

There is always fear. It may be fear of inadequacy, (Moses said, "*I am slow of speech and slow if tongue.*"), or maybe fear of failure, (the spies cried, "*The land we explored devours those living in it. All the people we saw there are of great size,*"). God will always be strong in our weakness. He promises His presence will be with you, and He will help you. "*So do not fear, for I am with you; do not be dismayed, for I am your God. I will strengthen you and help you; I will uphold you with my righteous right hand.*"[22]

Positioned to Proclaim the Gospel of the Kingdom

"And this gospel of the kingdom will be preached in the whole world as a testimony to all nations, and then the end will come."
– Matthew 24:14

"From one man he made all the nations, that they should inhabit the whole earth; and he marked out their appointed times in history and the boundaries of their lands. God did this so that they would seek him and perhaps reach out for him and find him, though he is not far from any one of us."[23]

As Creator of heaven and earth, all nations, and all people groups, God determined our times and places of habitation. He has established the exact dates for the rise and fall of kingdoms and empires. The purpose for this divine positioning is so that we would seek Him. The good news is that we don't have to grope around in the dark looking for God. He has done all this, so that we will look for him, reach out and find him.

We have been positioned to share the gospel wherever we live and in whatever sphere of influence is given to us. God has set the boundaries of our habitation. It is not a coincidence where God has placed you. Where you live and work is no accident. Each one of you has been positioned to share the gospel of the kingdom with your family, friends, neighbors, and co-workers within your sphere of influence.

I think we all want to know that we're on the right path. Whether your sphere of influence is in religion, media, government, education, business, family, or arts and entertainment, we all desire the assurance of being able to say, "I was created for this. I'm doing what God wants me to do."

God is calling women to a greater purpose than themselves. We are called and destined to lead cities, states, and nations, corporations, businesses, churches, and even become judges, senators, doctors and lawyers. He has given you specific gifts, talents, and abilities, and assigned you to distinct areas of influence to take territory for the Kingdom of God. Always be who you are and act in accordance with the gifting God has given you. He promises to do exceedingly abundantly above all that we could ever ask or imagine. He has truly done that for me.

"But God chose the foolish things of the world to shame the wise; God chose the weak things of the world to shame the strong. God chose the lowly things of this world and the despised things—and the things that are not—to nullify the things that are." [24]

ENDNOTES

1. "Moed," Strong's Hebrew 4150, *BibleHub.com*, Web. March 26, 2017, http://biblehub.com/str/hebrew/4150.htm.
2. Exodus 9:1-5
3. Ibid.
4. Genesis 12:1-2 AMP
5. Genesis 28:15
6. Jude 1:3
7. Isaiah 43:18-19
8. Genesis 19:16-26
9. Ibid.
10. Luke 17:32
11. Ruth 1:16-17
12. Proverbs 15:22-23
13. Romans 8:29
14. 2 Corinthians 3:4-5
15. Ephesians 1:17
16. Exodus 15:26
17. Isaiah 41:10
18. Philippians 3:10-11 MSG
19. Matthew 19:26
20. 2 Corinthians 1:20 MEV
21. Hebrews 4:12
22. Isaiah 41:10
23. Acts 17:26-27
24. 1 Corinthians 1:27-28

Chapter 9
WOMEN OF THE BIBLE

The Bible contains stories about women, some of their names we know, others we don't. Their stories range from unpleasant and devastating to encouraging and inspiring. We have the privilege of reading how they faced their circumstances, dealt with tragedy, navigated being marginalized, led nations, even being chosen to carry God's son. Because they are in the Bible, it may seem that they were more than mere humans, but just like us, they were limited to flesh and blood as well. Let's take a look at a few of them and reflect on their lives.

The Truth About Eve

Since the beginning of time, Satan has perverted our identity as women. Satan's goal is to misrepresent or distort your view of God to hinder your view of yourself and prevent you from seeing yourself as God sees you. One day, the Lord spoke to me and said, "See yourself as who you really are, and not as others see you." This was enlightening because I'd never truly considered how I was viewed in heaven.

Often, we don't see ourselves as God sees us. Perhaps like Mary, we think *"How will this be?"*[1] when the angel Gabriel informed her she would give birth to the Son of God. We can think of a lot of reasons why not because we feel unworthy or rationalize that what we've seen in the Spirit is just our imagination. When you believe the lies of Satan or your own vain imagination and reasoning, you will not come into the full knowledge of your true identity in Christ. You will have a distorted view of who you are and the world around you. Belief in Satan's lies will cause you to have an identity crisis, and to doubt what God has spoken over your life.

Understanding our true identity in Christ gives us purpose. God has a specific purpose for each one of us whether its's in or outside of the home. God's purposes and plans include all of us, male and female. The body of Christ misses out when we attempt to force all women into one constrained role.

Women are trailblazers. Today, women have made many contributions throughout history to our society. Women establish businesses, lead major corporations, start ministries, raise up godly children, and more. God is using women to advance His Kingdom in the earth. A woman's place should be valued, whether it's in the home, church, business, government, media, or whatever sphere of influence she has been given. What I discovered about my identity in Christ has bought me tears of joy, and at times sadness, when I think of how Satan has stolen the identity of many women today.

Eve's Story

Often when the story of Adam and Eve is read, it brings about negative thoughts and images with nothing good to say about the whole unpleasant incident, or about Eve. Yet there's more to the story than meets the eye. Eve's desire is misplaced. She is deceived because she doesn't know Satan is lying to her. Satan tricks her into believing that God is holding out on her and Adam, so they eat of the forbidden fruit in the garden. They are expelled from their garden home because of their disobedience. If Satan can get your mind twisted about who God is and the trustworthiness of His character, then he has you. What happened to Eve could happen to any one of us. We've all been gullible at times and may have listened to the father of lies, causing us to mistrust our Heavenly Father's words.

The Bible says that we all have the propensity to be deceived just as Eve when we take our eyes off of Jesus and fix them on other things. "*But I am afraid that just as Eve was deceived by the serpent's cunning, your minds may somehow be led astray from your sincere and pure devotion to Christ.*"[2]

2 Timothy reminds us about the evil that will be prevalent in the last days and false teachers who "*worm their way into homes and gain control over gullible women, who are loaded down with sins and are swayed by all kinds of evil desires.*"[3] Our desires must remain pure; otherwise we can get caught up in "*the lust of the flesh, the lust of the eyes, and the pride of life*" just as Eve did.[4] The world system can only offer a craving for physical pleasure, everything we see, and pride in our personal achievements and possessions. Yet our Heavenly Father offers so much more.

Eve Was Created for More

We've all heard disparaging comments that cast Eve as a "bad" person. Yet when God created Eve He said it was very good. When we only see Eve's sinful nature, we neglect to see the truth about Eve and God's Divine design for her and womankind.

In Genesis Chapter 2:18, after God forms man from the dust of the earth and placed him in the Garden of Eden, God says, "*It is not good for the man to be alone. I will make a helper suitable for him.*" What is God's solution? To make a "helper suitable" for the man. When God creates Eve, he calls her *ezer*—literally, a "life saver."[5] The word translated "*helper*" is the Hebrew term "*ezer.*" Now mind you, Satan is the father of lies who perverts what God intended for good.

The term "*helper*" doesn't mean housewife. While there is nothing wrong with being a housewife, it is not what this term expresses. When we understand God's purpose when He created Eve, we come to see the role of women on this earth in a much different light. I now better understand why God said finding a wife was a good thing.

Eve is not designed to be like Adam. The role of helper was not meant to be subservient to the man nor to usurp his authority. The Bible says, "*and the two will become one flesh. So they are no longer two, but one flesh.*"[6] In other words, they complement one another.

The phrase "*helper suitable,*" rendered "*help meet*" in the King James Version, comes from a combination of the words *ezer* and *kenegdo.* The Hebrew term "*ezer,*" or "*helper,*" is used elsewhere in Scripture to describe God:

- He is a *helper* to the fatherless – Psalm 10:14
- Israel's *shield* and *helper* – Deuteronomy 33:29
- David's *helper* and *deliverer* – Psalm 70:5
- God as *savior, rescuer,* or *protector* – Exodus 18:14, Deuteronomy. 33:7

Adam was alone, and God's solution was an *ezer kenegdo.* One couldn't be found in the rest of creation, so God made one. God is good. He always provides for the needs of His children.

Together, male and female reflect the image of God. They are both "mankind," while Adam reflects the more "masculine" characteristics of God and Eve the more "feminine." Eve is not created to be "the little helper." She is created to walk with Adam and fulfill God's command to have dominion over the earth. Eve is not made as an inferior being in any degree, but with a different and equally important role and purpose in life. One time, while I was overseeing the administration of the ministry I served, I overheard a male leader call me "the little Mrs." I must admit, I was offended at the time because I felt that this individual viewed me as inferior in my role and was mocking my authority and ability to lead and oversee the responsibilities that had been given to me. Today, I just chuckle at the thought in light of the spiritual authority granted God's daughters to make a significant impact for His purpose in many spheres of influence to destroy the works of the enemy.

Eve's deception led to our vulnerability to be deceived. Her choice to take the forbidden fruit from the tree of the knowledge of good and evil bought pain into the lives of every woman—specifically pain during childbirth and pain in our relationships. Fellowship with God was broken when Adam and Eve sinned in the garden. What Satan disguised as an opportunity turned out to be evil that had an impact on all of mankind.

Is it possible that because of Eve's sin we overlook the significance of why God created women? All women, were created in the image of God for His glory. God made you to resemble specific aspects of Him. He designed each of you uniquely. You represent Him in this world.

Abigail, a Wise and Determined Woman

As I was studying the term "ezer *kenegdo*," the story of Abigail, which you can read about in 1 Samuel 25, came to mind. Abigail is the wife of a wealthy man named Nabal who is foolish, intemperate, and mean. Nabal is a strange character, to say the least. His name, which means "fool" or 'foolish," also describes his character.[7] For no apparent reason, Nabal refuses David's request for food and shelter for his men and David does not take this rejection very well.

Abigail understands her role as an *"ezer kenegdo."* Abigail is not only intelligent and beautiful, she is also wise. She acts with discretion and saves her husband and her household by preventing David from doing something rash, and secures an unexpected future for herself. She becomes the third wife of King David after Nabal's death.[8] Daughters, you are beloved by God, and He has a plan for you. It should be your desire to reflect God and bring glory to Him since that was His original plan. You are loved! My hope is that you will gain new insight into your true identity in Christ and how much God values women. I hope that you will strive for the highest standards in whatever walk of life you find yourself, be it personal or professional. Your contribution is unique. God has given you talents you may not have identified. The Lord is calling you into His Service.

Other Notable Women of the Bible

The Bible is full of notable women: queens, prophetesses, a judge, the mother of Jesus, notable disciples of Jesus, and associates of Paul. Some women even have books of the Bible named after them. Others share the spotlight with their also-famous husbands or sons. You can probably name quite a few of these women.

Yet, there are less notable women who could be considered nobodies in the eyes of man that are mentioned in both the Old and New Testament. Many of these women held a supporting part in God's story. Who are some of these women? Let's delve into the Bible and learn from a few of these remarkable women.

The Wise Woman of Tekoa – 2 Samuel 14:1-21

Absalom has been banished by his father, King David, after murdering his brother Amnon for the assault of his sister, Tamar. Absalom is the eldest son of King David and Tamar's full brother. Amnon is their half-brother. Joab, King David's nephew, knows David loves and misses his son. Joab thinks of a way of bringing Absalom back home. He sends someone to Tekoa to find a "wise woman." Joab instructs her how to dress and what to say.

So, the "wise woman" comes to see King David, pretending to seek protection in her own family feud. The woman says that her son killed his brother, and now the rest of the family wants to kill him. This woman is rather bold and convincing. Her made-up story parallels David's real story of Absalom killing Amon and then fleeing to another country. She then turns the tables and challenges King David to bring Absalom back. When David decides that her son should be spared and promises to provide protection for her, the Tekoite woman tells him that he should also spare Absalom. God used this wise woman to accomplish His purpose to restore King David and Absalom's relationship.

The Widow of Zarephath – 1 Kings 17:7-24

The prophet Elijah shows up during a time of famine and asks this woman to fix him lunch. Sadly, the widow is in need herself. She explains that she only has enough for one last meal for herself and her son before they die of starvation. Elijah's answer is certainly a test of her faith. He tells her that she is to make some food for him anyway and promises her that *"her jar of flour will not be used up and the jug of oil will not run dry until the day the Lord sends rain on the land."* She uses her last provisions to make him some bread. Miraculously, they aren't her last provisions. Her flour and oil last until the end of the drought. Her remarkable faith is tested again when her son dies. Elijah brings him back to life.

The Poor Widow with the Olive Oil – 2 Kings 4:1-7

Elisha is the prophetic successor of Elijah, and performs exploits similar as his predecessor. A widow, the wife of one of the sons of the prophets, is having trouble paying her late husband's debts. A creditor threatens to take her two sons as slaves. All she owns is a small bottle of olive oil. Elisha tells her to borrow as many jars as possible from her neighbors and fill them all with the oil from her bottle. She obeys the prophet. Amazingly, the oil keeps pouring until every jar is filled. She then begins selling the oil to pay her debts. Sometimes God wants us to step out in faith just as this woman did. When we look at our resources and abilities, we might shrink away from such an act of faith. Yet, when we obey in faith, God provides.

The Woman with the Issue of Blood – Mark 5:25-34

This woman had suffered a great deal under the care of many doctors and had spent all that she had. Instead of getting better, she grew worse. Jesus is rushing to heal someone else when this woman pushes through the crowd and touches His clothes. She believes that the mere contact with Him will cure her of the hemorrhaging that had plagued her for twelve years. Amazingly, despite the throng around Him, Jesus stops and asks who touched Him. When the woman comes forward and kneels before Him, He makes the impersonal personal by saying, "*Daughter, you are now well because of your faith.*" It is not the touch of some magic garment that healed her, but her trust in the Healer.

The Poor but Generous Widow – Luke 21:1-4

There was a collection box in the Temple, where people could make donations. Jesus sees a poor widow put two very small copper coins in the offering. Jesus exalts her over the wealthy people making a big show of their offerings by saying, "*this poor widow has put in more than all the others. All these people gave their gifts out of their wealth; but she out of her poverty put in all she had to live on.*"

Mary of Bethany, the Sinful Woman
Who Anointed Jesus' Feet – Luke 7:36-50

Jesus is invited to dine with the Pharisees. During the meal, a woman named Mary enters. Without welcome from the Pharisees, she sits down at Jesus' feet, "*wipe[s] them with her hair, kiss[es] them and pour[s] perfume on them.*" The Pharisees are offended by the "sinner" in their presence. This is considered a scandalous act. A woman entering a house where men are dining without an invitation was considered highly inappropriate.

Why did she go about this in such a scandalous way? At first glance, it appeared that she "wasted" a jar of expensive perfume. She uncovered her head, then wiped the dirt and dust off Jesus' feet with her hair! Simon, one of the Pharisees who invited Jesus, said to himself that if Jesus were a prophet He would know a sinner was touching Him. Jesus made it clear that Mary's sins had been forgiven and her faith saved her.

As I read the accounts of these women and their encounters with Jesus, I sense the Father's love revealed through the faith stories of these women. He sees our brokenness and has compassion for us. How He longs to forgive, reconcile, and restore women to their rightful inheritance in His Kingdom. When you have been touched by the Father, you can't help but be changed forever.

Harlots in the Bible

It's been said that prostitution is the oldest profession in the world. The Bible speaks of prostitution and harlots in both the Old and New Testaments. Maybe you wonder why I chose to write about the *harlots* in the Bible? Simply put, God desires to bring restoration to all women in this season, including prostitutes. He wants to bring salvation, healing, and deliverance to all. So many women find themselves trying to fit into society's mold, and when they don't seem to fit, they seek other avenues to feel valued—even destructive ones.

As I was researching for the book, I saw that there are different kinds of prostitutes found in biblical stories. First, there are those who offered to have sex with men to earn money or to get some personal favor. Some women may have become prostitutes to survive when they no longer were under the protection or care of a husband, father, or other family members. There were also "sacred" or "temple" prostitutes, a female or a male who had sex with worshipers of a god or goddess in a temple. Many of these gods or goddesses were thought to make the land and its people fertile.[10]

In the Old Testament, Israel's unfaithfulness is often compared with being a prostitute or chasing after prostitutes. In Revelation 17, the writer calls Babylon, meaning the Roman Empire, a shameless prostitute who tempts people and nations into relations with her.

The Law of Moses forbade prostitution, and those found guilty could be killed by crushing them with stones, a priest's daughter who became a prostitute was to be burned to death, and no money earned by prostitutes was to be accepted as a gift to the temple. They were to be completely rejected.

Sorrowfully, this still occurs today in many parts of the world. Women prostitute themselves for various reasons. Many women give away their precious bodies for money or the lure of having a committed relationship. Young girls and boys are trafficked for sex by selfish people. Yet despite all of this, God still loves them. Ezekiel 16 depicts the history of Jerusalem from God's experience as the Husband of an adulterous wife. God expresses His love in Ezekiel 16:18 saying:

> *"Later I passed by, and when I looked at you and saw that you were old enough for love, I spread the corner of my garment over you and covered your naked body. I gave you my solemn oath and entered into a covenant with you, declares the Sovereign Lord, and you became mine."*

When I read this, my heart melts just knowing the magnitude of God's love for people. How often do we pass by and give others the evil eye because of their perceived wrongdoing and shortcomings? As believers, when we receive salvation, our sins are forgiven and covered by the Blood of Jesus. We are encouraged to *"above all, love each other deeply because, love covers a multitude of sin."*[11] Most importantly, no matter what condition a person is in, God's love should prevail over sin.

Yes, Jesus loves prostitutes. While prostitutes are not living within God's will for their lives, they are not outside of His grace and mercy. Matthew 21:31 says, "*Truly I tell you, the tax collectors and the prostitutes are entering the kingdom of God ahead of you.*"

Who was Jesus speaking to? The chief priests and the elders (religious people). Why did He tell them this? Because the tax collectors and harlots believed John the Baptist when he came preaching the way of righteousness, and they did not.

Throughout history, God has used women, including prostitutes, to fulfill many of his most strategic purposes. Many of them were unlikely choices, yet God chose to use them despite their shortcomings and moral failures. These women took risks. I don't know what made these women different and willing to take extraordinary risks in volatile times. Perhaps it was out of necessity and hope for a better future.

The first notable mention of a harlot occurs in Genesis 38. Tamar, a widow of Er and Onan, plays the prostitute to get pregnant by her father-in-law Judah (patriarch of the line of Judah). I recall the first time I read her story years ago. My eyes lit up because I had no idea that God would use such a person to reveal His divine purpose. Yet, her story could be our story. Tamar is vindicated soon after their encounter when Judah learns of Tamar's pregnancy. Judah orders his tribesmen to bring her out to be burned because prostitution was illegal. When Judah demands to know who had fathered her child, Tamar calls him out, letting him know that he is the man who fathered her child. She provides proof, producing Judah's signet, belt, and staff that she had taken during her encounter with him on a dusty road. Judah acknowledges that by the Levirate custom (law), [13] which decreed that a widow should, or in rare cases must, marry her dead husband's brother. Tamar had been right to seek pregnancy through her father-in-law in order to continue the line of her husband Er. By doing so, she fulfilled her duty to her husband and her family, and helped fulfill God's promise to Abraham of many descendants. Tamar was forgiven and returned to her father-in-law's family. Tamar is honored by being in the lineage of Jesus.

Tamar is not the only harlot in the Bible with important descendants. In the second chapter of Joshua, two Hebrew spies lodge in the house of a harlot named Rahab while in Jericho. She hides them in return for their promise that when they invade her city, she and her family will be spared. Joshua keeps the agreement, and Rahab, and her family are spared. She is also honored by being in the lineage of Jesus.

As mentioned in an earlier chapter, Gomer is the prostitute Hosea married when God told him to pick a whore for a wife. There are also other less notable prostitutes in the Bible, as in the story of Jephthah, a judge over Israel for six years whose mother is a harlot.

As believers, we are called to be a light in a dark world and to step out of our comfort zone and be face-to-face with daily opportunities to live the gospel, no matter where we live. Rather than being moved with compassion, we often shun the thought of coming into contact with those the world would describe as unlovable. We spout off phrases like "loving the unlovely" or "Jesus was a friend of sinners," which sound godly, but faith without works is dead. We pride ourselves on being righteous, but the Bible says, "*all our righteous acts are like filthy rags.*"

Women in Hebrews Hall of Faith

Hebrews 11 is described as the Hall of Faith. These heroes and heroines of the Bible made a significant impact in helping to fulfill God's redemptive plan. Several are women who boldly and bravely displayed their confidence in God and made enormous differences in the Kingdom.

Sarah – "*By faith even Sarah, who was past childbearing age, was enabled to bear children because she considered him faithful who had made the promise.*" – Hebrews 11:11

Sarah trusts GOD in His promises and conceives a son even in her old age. There are even times when Abraham caves in to fear. Once, when He journeys into Egypt, he says that she is his sister. Abraham is afraid that the Egyptians would see just how beautiful Sarah was and kill him to take her as Pharaoh's own.

Rahab – "*By faith the prostitute Rahab, because she welcomed the spies, was not killed with those who were disobedient.*" – Hebrews 11:31

Rahab risks her life by hiding the twelve spies of Israel when Moses sent them to spy out the land of Canaan. In Joshua 2:1 we read that "*Joshua son of Nun secretly sent two spies from Shittim. "Go, look over the land," he said, "especially Jericho. So they went and entered the house of a prostitute named Rahab and stayed there.*" Somehow, Rahab knows that God had given the land to the nation of Israel. Joshua spares Rabab, and she is considered righteous for having given lodging to the spies. In so doing, Rahab later becomes part of the royal lineage of King David and of Jesus Christ.

The Story of Queen Esther: A Portrait of Grace, Courage, Strength, and Dignity

I have always been fascinated with Queen Esther's story. You probably already know the story, because it's a classic. Esther, born Hadassah, is one of the great women of the Bible. Hadassah is a Hebrew name meaning "myrtle, a myrtle tree."[14] The myrtle tree's leaves releases a sweet fragrance when crushed. It reminds me that "*we are to God the pleasing aroma of Christ among those who are being saved and those who are perishing.*"[15]

Esther's Jewish identity is hidden for many years. Esther grows up without her parents. What I have learned over the years is that life's circumstances can either make us bitter or better, but it is obvious through Esther's story, she chooses the latter. Her story has great relevance to our lives as women today. Even though she is an ancient Jewish queen, we can all learn from her wisdom and humility.

King Xerxes is the king of the greatest empire in the world of his day. His powerful empire spread from India to Cush which is the upper Nile region.[16] Esther 1:3 tells us that *"in the third year of his reign he gave a banquet for all his nobles and officials. The military leaders of Persia and Media, the princes, and the nobles of the provinces were present."* King Xerxes, displays the vast wealth of his kingdom and the splendor and glory of his majesty for 180 days. When these days are over, the king gives a banquet that lasted seven days.

Queen Vashti is the first wife of King Xerxes. She is described as a beautiful woman. In fact, her name means "beautiful woman" in Persian.[17] She must have been one of the loveliest women in the realm of King Xerxes, who thinks so much of his wife's physical charms that he wants to show off her beauty. In her own right, she possesses both strength and beauty.

The reputation of King Xerxes is not flawless. He is known to be an impulsive and headstrong man. As the extended 180-day feast in the palace of the king progresses, it ultimately dissolves into drunken excess. In Esther 1:11, the king calls Queen Vashti to appear before him *"in order to display her beauty to the people and nobles, for she was lovely to look at."* However, Queen Vashti refuses to come before the king and his men. She does not want to become a public spectacle, and King Xerxes is enraged. At the advice of his trusted counselors, he decides to remove her by royal decree—the law of the Medes and the Persians which could never be reversed, not even by the king himself.[18] It's important to know that these laws are irrevocable and can never be altered. That meant Vashti can no longer come before the king, and that her royal position is to be given to another.

"Later when King Xerxes' fury had subsided, he remember[s] Vashti and what she had done and what he had decreed about her."[19] But it is too late. His decree is irreversible. That is when his aides suggest an all-Persia beauty contest to find a queen for King Xerxes.

Mordecai, a Jew of the tribe of Benjamin, has a cousin named Hadassah, also called Esther, whom he had bought up because she did not have a mother or father. She has a lovely figure and is beautiful. Mordecai instructs Esther not to reveal her nationality and family background to protect her. Many young women, including Esther, are bought to the citadel of Susa (the king's palace) and put under the care of Hegai. Esther wins the favor of Hegai, who has her receive special beauty treatments and food. He also assigns Esther seven female attendants selected from the king's palace and moves her and her attendants into the best place in the harem. Esther receives royal treatment even before she marries the king.

Esther has to complete twelve months of beauty treatments that were arranged for the women, six months with oil of myrrh and six with perfumes and cosmetics. Imagine being transformed and immersed in the perfect spa treatments. When it comes time for Esther to come before the king, she does not ask for anything other than what Hegai suggested. Esther wins the favor of everyone who sees her.

King Xerxes is attracted to Esther more than any of the other women. She wins his favor and approval. So, he sets a royal crown on her head and makes her the queen over Vashti. Esther is chosen! She is crowned queen in place of Vashti. King Xerxes holds a big dinner in Esther's honor. He makes the day a holiday and gave away expensive gifts. She is now married to a man who doesn't even know her godly heritage as a Jew or Israelite.

God Uses Esther to Save His People

> *"Haman was a very important man in Persia. He was an evil man who plotted to destroy the Jews. Haman wanted Mordecai to bow down to him also. But Mordecai won't do it. Haman was enraged. So, he looked for a way to destroy all Mordecai's people, the Jews." – Esther 3:6*

When Mordecai learns of Haman's plot to kill the Jews, he goes into mourning. Mordecai tears his clothes, puts on sack cloth and ashes, and walks into the city crying out loud. When Queen Esther's eunuchs and female attendants come and tell her about Mordecai, she is in great distress. Queen Esther sends clothes for him to put on instead of his sackcloth, but Mordecai will not accept them. So, Queen Esther sends one of the king's eunuchs assigned to attend her to find out what is troubling Mordecai. Mordecai tells him everything that had happened and gives him a copy of the official order for the destruction of the Jews. Mordecai tells the eunuch to instruct Queen Esther to go into the king's presence to beg for mercy and plead with him for her people.

Following this instruction, Queen Esther sends word to Mordecai that for any man or woman who approaches the king in the inner court without being summoned the king has but one law, "*that they be put to death unless the king extends the gold scepter to them and spares their lives.*"[20] Mordecai responds to Queen Esther:

> "*Do not think that because you are in the king's house you alone of all the Jews will escape. For if you remain silent at this time, relief and deliverance for the Jews will arise from another place, but you and your father's family will perish. And who knows but that you have come to your royal position for such a time as this?*"[21]

What does Queen Esther do? She calls for a fast among her people and said, "*When this is done, I will go to the king, even though it is against the law. And if I perish, I perish*"[22] On the third day, Queen Esther puts on her royal robes and stands in the inner court of the palace. When the king sees her standing in the court, he holds out the golden scepter and asks her what she wants. Esther requests that the king and Haman attend a banquet.

At that banquet Esther tells the king, "*If I have found favor with you, Your*

Majesty, and if it pleases you, grant me my life—this is my petition. And spare my people—this is my request."[23] King Xerxes asks Queen Esther, "Who is the man that would do such a thing?" Queen Esther tells him that it is Haman. Now the king is angry. He commands that Haman be killed. Afterward, the king makes Mordecai second in power only to himself. Mordecai then sees to it that a new law allows the Jews to fight for their lives on the day they are supposed to be killed. Because Mordecai is such an important man now, many people help the Israelites, and they are saved from their enemies.

Esther was chosen for that specific time and place. Her physical beauty was a device used by God to achieve His sovereign purposes. It was Esther's divine destiny to become an ambassador for the kingdom of heaven at a critical time in the history of Israel.

I believe some of the strongest and greatest heroines of the faith are laboring in love for the Lord today. They are wives, mothers, grandmas, sisters, daughters, and perhaps former prostitutes. Their life story is like reading stories of the past, right out of the Bible. Many may be unnoticed or rejected by the world, but they are never unnoticed or rejected by God.

ENDNOTES

1. Luke 1:34

2. 2 Corinthians 11:3

3. 2 Timothy 3:6

4. 1 John 2:16

5. "Ezer Kenegdo", *Ransom Heart*, Web. July 2, 2017, https://www.ransomedheart.com/daily-reading/ezer-kenegdo.

6. Mark 10:38

7. "Nabal", Easton's Bible Dictionary – Nabal, *Bible Study Tools,* Web. July 2, 2017, http://www.biblestudytools.com/dictionary/nabal/.

8. 1 Samuel 25:18

9. 1 Kings 17:7-12

10. 'Cush", Esther 1:1, That is, the upper Nile region, Biblegateway, Web. July 4, 2017, https://www.biblegateway.com/passage/?search=Esther+1.

11. 1 Peter 4L8

12. Isaiah 64:6

13. Levirate, *Britannica,* Encyclopedia Britannica, Web. July 25, 2017, https://www.britannica.com/topic/levirate

14. "Myrtle," Origin of the name Hadassah, *Baby Names*, Web, July 2, 2017, http://www.babynamewizard.com/baby-name/girl/hadassah

15. 2 Corinthians 2:15

16. 'Cush", Esther 1:1 That is, the upper Nile region, *Biblegateway*, Web. July 4, 2017, https://www.biblegateway.com/passage/?search=Esther+1

17. "Vashti, She Knows, Web. July 4, 2017, http://www.sheknows.com/baby-names/name/vashti.

18. "Law of the Medes and Persians", *oxforddictionaries.com,* English Oxford Dictionary, Web. July 4, 2017, https://en.oxforddictionaries.com/definition/law_of_the_medes_and_persians.

19. Esther 2:1

20. Esther 4:4-16

21. Ibid

22. Ibid

23. Esther 7:3

Chapter 10

PRINCESS WARRIOR

Deborah – Destined to Lead a Nation

I love the story of Deborah in the Book of Judges. Something awakens inside of me each time I read the story of this brave woman. This Princess Warrior was chosen by God to be a leader at an unlikely time in her day.

Deborah's role is impressive. She is a prophetess, judge, counselor, warrior, the wife of Lapidoth, and mother of Israel. Deborah leads Israel, seeing to the affairs of the people. Deborah is a righteous judge. She holds court under the Palm of Deborah in the hill country between Ramah and Bethel. The Israelites come to her to have their disputes settled.

The back story of what is going on at that time begins with how the Israelites are doing evil in the sight of the Lord, now that Ehud is dead. Ehud is a judge sent by God to deliver the Israelites from Moabite domination. Israel has fallen into trouble because of their own sin. Because the Israelites are doing evil in the eyes of the Lord, He sells them into the hands of Jabin king of Canaan. Sisera, the commander of his army, cruelly oppresses the Israelites for twenty years. The Israelites cry out to the Lord for help. God hears the Israelites cry and raises up Deborah to intervene in the plight of His children.

Divine Strategy and Marching Orders

Deborah sends for Barak and says to him, "*The Lord, the God of Israel, commands you: 'Go, take with you ten thousand men of Naphtali and Zebulun and lead them up to Mount Tabor.*"[1] Deborah, a woman of strength and faith, is anointed to deliver God's marching orders to Barak. However, in Judges 4:4-15 we see that Barak says to her, "*If you go with me, I will go; but if you don't go with me, I won't go.*" Deborah responds, "*Certainly I will go with you.*" Deborah says to Barak that the honor will not be his because the Lord will deliver Sisera into the hands of a woman.

Barak is not a weak or timid man. He is a mature, strong, and proven commander. He immediately submits to Deborah's authority and prophetic insight. Deborah and Barak gathers 10,000 troops and attack Sisera and his army. The Lord has given His word that He would lure Sisera and the army of Jabin into his midst, enabling Barak to accomplish his mission.

I wonder what Deborah must have felt when she first learned she was called to lead a nation. Did she cower at the thought? Did she wonder why God called her for such a task? Did she feel inadequate?

Vision, Wisdom, Courage and Passion

Deborah teamed up with Barak to change her nation. God did not call her to an easy task. In fact, it was a rather impossible one. Can you relate? Have you have been called by God to do something you feel totally inadequate to do? What can we learn from Deborah's leadership style by putting aside our personal agendas and listening for God's clear direction? Many times, as Christian women we don't stand together. We neglect to realize that by forming alliances against evil we can change and reform nations. Together we can do what no lone voice can when we join forces to bring change to our communities for righteousness sake.

Deborah's example admonishes us to always remember and respect the power of a woman ordained by God for His purposes. Many years ago, the Lord revealed to me that the Deborahs of God are arising, through the book, *The Deborah Company*, by Jane Hamon. In my head I said, "Father, you have got to be kidding me. There is no way I can do this. I feel so inadequate." Now more than ever this has become very real to me.

God's daughters will break many barriers. We must have the ability to clearly hear God's voice, and become women of wisdom and understanding. Here's the truth, when women rise up in faith we will feed the poor, take care of the widows and the orphans, help the homeless, preach the good news, and help eradicate poverty. We will free women bound in domestic violence, drug abuse, bad relationships, human sex trafficking, and prostitution in a profound way.

God is calling ordinary women to come alongside Him do extraordinary work. Make no mistake about it, embracing the call will not be easy or glamorous. We may have to take off our stilettos, diamonds and pearls, put on our combat boots and roll up our sleeves, because the lives of our loved ones and the lost are worth so much more.

As the Lord begins to lead us to embrace our calling and the stirring in our heart for His destiny and purpose, we will begin to sense a divine urgency and responsibility for things greater than ourselves. I encourage you to take up the sword of the Spirit which is the Word of God, and seek divine revelation, wisdom and strategies that will make an impact in your homes and your communities.

Jesus has already given us the command to "Go." To step out fearlessly into battle, lifting high the banner of our King, declaring that the victory belongs to Him. So, will you war with prayer? Will you war with your actions of kindness and your words of love? Will you step out and love the un-lovable? Will you share the Gospel, comfort the hurting, and help dispel the darkness?

Rise up, women of faith! If He did it before, He can do it again. Catch the vision of what God is doing in the lives of women in the body of Christ so that we can work together to effectively fulfill His Kingdom purposes here on earth. Let's take back what the enemy has stolen from us. It's time to rise in faith. I hear the Lord saying, "Rise up with the spirit of Deborah, under the anointing and grace!"

Jael – An Ordinary Woman with the Heart of a Lioness

Sisera is a real threat to Israel and engages them in battle. As the battle ensues, Barak pursues the chariots and all of Sisera's troops fall by the sword. Sisera flees on foot and staggers into Jael's camp. Sisera has no way of knowing that Jael is the women that will fulfill the prophetic words God gave to Deborah regarding the victory.

Jael goes out to meet Sisera. She calls him into her tent, hides him and feeds him. Then Jael murders him in his sleep, fulfilling Deborah's prophecy. Jael is the heroine who kills Sisera to deliver Israel from the troops of King Jabin. Afterwards, Israel experiences 40 years of peace because of her lion-hearted act.

Our God is a warrior. He uses the title "Lord of hosts" or "Lord of armies" in the Bible. Exodus 15:3 says, "*The LORD is a warrior; the LORD is his name.*" Isaiah 42:13 says, "*The LORD will march out like a champion, like a warrior he will stir up his zeal; with a shout he will raise the battle cry and will triumph over his enemies.*"

Daughter, you are a "*princess warrior.*" You are adopted as a child of the King and made in the very image of God Himself. He has clothed you with garments of salvation and arrayed you in a robe of His righteousness.[2]

The whole thought of a "*princess warrior*" was foreign to me, but one day in 2016 the Lord spoke these words into my spirit. When I first heard the concept "*princess warrior,*" I could see how being a daughter makes me a princess, but a "*warrior*"? Honestly, I never saw myself as a "*warrior.*" I only wanted to serve the Lord in "*good faith.*"

Every little girl's dream is to be a princess, to wear fancy dresses, sparkly shoes and a beautiful jeweled adorned tiara, and to someday marry her prince charming in a fairytale wedding. *Merriam Webster* defines princess as a woman having sovereign power; a female member of a royal family; especially: a daughter or granddaughter of a sovereign.[3] We are daughters of the King, making us princesses with a new identity.

As God's daughters, we have not been given a spirit of fear. The call to follow Christ and become a "*warrior*" in His Kingdom requires fierceness. Jesus said, "*From the days of John the Baptist until now, the kingdom of heaven has been subjected to violence, and violent people have been raiding it.*"[4]

Did you know that being a warrior is a part of God's design? A warrior is a person engaged in struggle or conflict. A princess warrior is not afraid to pick up her cross and follow Christ. She knows that to live is Christ, and to die is gain, and is willing to give what she cannot keep, to gain what she cannot lose. She wakes up every morning prepared for battle, waging war against sin and death so that all might come to life in Christ. She is fearless. Unafraid, she boldly faces persecution, ridicule, and even suffering with unwavering faith and a steadfast heart.

The word *ezer,* mentioned earlier, is also used to refer to military power and strength, as well as to God himself as defender and protector.

- He is your shield and helper and your glorious sword (Deuteronomy 33:29).
- We wait and hope in the Lord, he is our help and shield (Psalm 33:20).
- You are my help and my deliverer; Lord, do not delay (Psalm 70:5).
- You who fear him, trust in the Lord, he is their help and shield (Psalm 115:9-11).
- I lift up my eyes to the mountains--where does my help come from? My help comes from the Lord, the Maker of heaven and earth (Psalm 121:1-2).

Fierce Women Prepare for Battle

Fierce women exude godly strength, courage, loyalty, and determination. Fierce women don't grovel for attention and aren't desperate to be seen. They don't depend on others for their identity or happiness. They are not loud, foul-mouthed, pushy, obnoxious, arrogant, self-centered, or demanding. They have tapped in fully to the forgiveness, grace and love of Christ. They have found true godly contentment in Him.

They are warriors at heart, having the mind of Christ and undaunted by life's challenges. They are not violent or aggressive, but tempered by humility and grace. Their identity and value are rooted in their relationship with Christ alone. They are passionate about things that matter rather than living for the trivial. These emerging *"princess warriors"* will have this resolve because they know who they are. They will impact and bring transformation not only to the body of Christ, but to nations. They are fearless warriors for the truth of the gospel. Luke 9:23-24 says, *"Whoever wants to be my disciple must deny themselves and take up their cross daily and follow me. For whoever wants to save their life will lose it, but whoever loses their life for me will save it."*

And yes, you will be tested. This woman has gone through the furnace of afflictions and came out as pure gold. And she's said YES to God. Isaiah 48:10 says, "*See, I have refined you, though not as silver; I have tested you in the furnace of affliction.*"

We must develop the character to fulfill our potential as God's warriors. We must grow in our ability to strengthen ourselves in the Lord. We must be able to strengthen and minister to ourselves and others. David had the ability to strengthen and encourage himself in the Lord. David had been seeking the Lord for years. He sought the Lord in the secret place when no one was watching. Like David, we must seek the Lord in the secret place. It is God's desire that we dwell in His presence. He wants to commune with us, take refuge in Him and give divine strategies for the battle.

There is a Battle Raging

Whether you realize it or not, you are in a battle. There is a battle raging between two kingdoms. The battle is fierce! We are in a spiritual war, a conflict between two kingdoms: the kingdoms of light and darkness. The war between these two kingdoms has been going on for quite some time and is still raging. Although the outcome of this war has already been predetermined before time began, we have been enlisted in the army of the Lord. The weapons of our warfare are not carnal weapons, but much more powerful. The divinely powerful weapons are spiritual for tearing down obstacles in the spiritual realm.

From the time of the resurrection of Christ, when the men hid in fear, women courageously went to His grave to seek Him. The women who went to His tomb remained faithful, even though it looked as if truth had been completely defeated. They were therefore blessed with the great honor to first take up the apostolic commission to be witnesses of His resurrection. Courageous women have always been on the front line of the battle between light and darkness, and will be so until the end. Women are arising and risking all for the sake of the gospel. Women will not have to become masculine to take their rightful place in His army. The Bible says, *"the people that do know their God shall be strong, and do exploits."*[5]

Two women in the Bible the Holy Spirit specifically impressed upon my spirit were Esther and Deborah. They were significant because I needed to see spiritually what God was doing in my life during that season of preparation to encourage me to continue on the path no matter how things looked. Using Esther, the Spirit revealed how she was hidden away in the palace (she could not reveal her identity) and had to undergo a process of preparation before being released into her destiny to save the Jewish nation. The Spirit also used the life of Deborah to reveal to me God's prophetic call on my life. Deborah carried an apostolic/prophetic anointing to bring change to a nation in turmoil.

It was difficult for me to comprehend that the Holy Spirit was not showing others what He was showing me. I was growing in the prophetic so I needed to understand that I had been hidden away for a specific time and purpose that was yet to be revealed. I soon learned through a prophetic training class that even though you may have some clue that you are a prophet, God still wants to hide you for the sake of understanding your purpose and the direction for your life. He wants you to know who you are, but doesn't want you to reveal your identity to anyone. He wants to hide you until He finishes working in you. This confirmed what God was doing in my life, but how would I know when God would be finished working in me? That was approximately nine years ago. He's not done with me yet, but I know the time is now!

Several years ago, the Lord impressed upon my spirit, "you are a part of My end-time army." All believers are called to be soldiers in the Lord's army. We may have different purpose and callings, but all should be engaged in the battle between good and evil, righteousness and sin, light and darkness, faith and unbelief, and in the end, God and Satan.

When I joined WIMN, almost a year ago, under the apostolic grace of Dr. Patricia King, a well-respected apostolic minister of the gospel, I receive a prophetic word of encouragement from Dr. Michelle Burkett that said, "*Francine (Aleatha)—you are an imparter of truth and a warrior who brings many to freedom—I hear Isaiah 45:2-3 over you today.*" "*This is what the Lord says: "I will go before you, Cyrus, and level the mountains. I will smash down gates of bronze and cut through bars of iron. And I will give you treasures hidden in the darkness—secret riches. I will do this so you may know that I am the Lord, the God of Israel, the one who calls you by name."* I never considered myself a warrior, yet this prophetic word changed my thinking. I didn't set out to become a warrior, but I choose to accept the assignment knowing the One who goes before me will pave the way, just as He has always done.

In 2017, I was ordained a minister through WIMN. I was given another prophetic word that also changed my life. It was prophesied that I had been given a "*justice mantle.*" This was "weighty" and foreign to me—a whole new reality. These prophetic words confirmed the truth of my identity in Christ and what the Lord had be revealing to me over the years. I am reminded of the call of Elisha the prophet when he received Elijah's mantle. Elijah found him plowing in the field with twelve pairs of oxen. Elijah went up to him and threw his cloak around him. Elisha then left his oxen and ran after Elijah. Elisha took his call seriously. He asked Elijah to let him kiss his father and mother goodbye to follow him. He counted the cost to obey the call. He didn't attempt to put off the call or hesitate. Once I said yes and accepted this mantle, my perspective, aspirations, goals, and priorities shifted. There was no looking back.

Mantles are established and destined by God. I had studied about mantles some years ago, yet never considered being given a specific mantle to make a difference in God's Kingdom. The Lord later gave me this scripture from Job 29:19, "*I put on righteousness as my clothing; justice was my robe and my turban.*" Just as the Father sent the Son, the Son is sending His daughters, in the power of His Spirit, to seek His righteous justice in the earth.

I can't say at this time I fully understand the assignment given to me. What I do know is, He will give clarity as I step forward to fulfill the mission. God never grants someone an assignment without giving him or her the ability to complete it. I trust God with my life and He has never failed me. Author Kris Vallotton says, "When God commissions leaders, as He did with Joshua, He releases mantles over them. These mantles give them the supernatural ability to complete their mission."[6] When God anoints us, He pours out His Spirit on us, empowering us to do what He calls us to do.

My heart's cry is "I want more of You, Lord." No matter what the cost, I want to align my life with the Holy Spirit's present movement. I encourage you to allow your hunger for more of God to move beyond familiarity and into destiny. Press past restrictions of religion and align your life with the continuous flow of the river of God that flows from Heaven.

I encourage you to prophesy to yourself about your destiny. Speak to the potential inside of you! Speak to those dormant seeds planted years ago and say, "SEED LIVE! Birth and bring forth. God knows the time and season to bring you forth. You have been called to serve the purposes of God in your generation. Be like Esther and Deborah, who were called in their season to save a nation. God has prepared you for such a time as this. You have been called to deliver a message to a dry and thirsty world! You have a precious message inside of you to be ministered in this season.

You are His daughter, made in His image, designed to defend your faith, your family, and your community. Rise up, Daughters of the King. God is calling you into battle!

You Were Made for More

The desperate need of this present hour is not merely for people who are trained and educated, but for people of God who are anointed, committed and willing to bring God's Kingdom to a hurting and desperate world through signs, wonders, and the power of the Holy Spirit.

We see from the many stories recorded throughout history that God has always desired to bring salvation, healing, and deliverance to people caught up in the ills of society. In our most unfortunate state, God loves us and will deliver us. It has always been God's plan to restore us to a place of dignity, self-worth, and wholeness. We are not defined by the world's standards. We are royalty. 1 Peter 2:9 says, *"But you are a chosen people, a royal priesthood, a holy nation, God's special possession."*

We have a rich heritage in Christ. We must carry ourselves as light in a dark world, vessels that have been broken and cleansed, and are willing to be filled with His Spirit and the Word. Women who speak the knowledge and wisdom of God are a rare jewel: *"Gold there is, and rubies are in abundance, but lips that speak knowledge are a rare jewel."*[7]

Father God is extending an invitation to His daughters to become a part of His story and to make a difference in His Kingdom to impact history. He is calling ordinary women like you and me to come alongside Him in what He is doing. Although your calling may not be on as grand a scale as Queen Esther or Deborah, it certainly is an opportunity to make a difference. You are called to release God's glory in the earth. We all have a gift to share. It doesn't have to be one of the five-fold ministries of apostles, prophets, evangelists, pastors, or teachers to make a difference in your sphere of influence.

Possessing Your Inheritance

When I became a born-again Christian, I became a new creation in Christ. Yet, nothing in my upbringing had prepared me for the destiny God had preplanned for me. Although I went to church, when I turned of age, I had no interest in God or religion. Like many, I was ready to venture out to find my place in the world. I had no idea what God had for me down the road. Things drastically changed when life's circumstances drew me into a sincere relationship with the King. Going after your destiny in God is a process that takes time. The Lord placed many people along my path to help guide me towards accomplishing His purpose in my life.

Women from all walks of life are taking hold of the inheritance God has planned for them. Like the daughters of Zelophehad, they are coming forward to claim their right to inherit the promise. All that we can think or desire in accordance with God's will is ours as part of our covenant of grace. Our heritage is exceedingly great and precious. Our inheritance is more than salvation and forgiveness of sins. Allow faith to arise in you, so that you are confident about your future. God has given us amazing promises for our future and for our children.

> *"In him we were also chosen, having been predestined according to the plan of him who works out everything in conformity with the purpose of his will, in order that we, who were the first to put our hope in Christ, might be for the praise of his glory. And you also were included in Christ when you heard the message of truth, the gospel of your salvation. When you believed, you were marked in him with a seal, the promised Holy Spirit, who is a deposit guaranteeing our inheritance until the redemption of those who are God's possession—to the praise of his glory."*[8]

We possess our inheritance through faith and patience. If we attempt to possess our inheritance before God's appointed time, we run the risk of missing out on the fullness of what God has promised. Hebrews 10:36 says, "*You have need of perseverance so that when you have done the will of God, you will receive what he has promised.*"

We must take our eyes off our problems and fix them on Jesus, who is the author and finisher of our faith. It's not easy and it takes discipline, but focusing on the troubles of our lives only diverts our attention away from God. We have an amazing example in Jesus, who endured the unimaginable to obtain the prize of redemption for us. Let's look to Jesus and focus on Him.

> "*Looking away [from all that will distract] to Jesus, Who is the Leader and the Source of our faith [giving the first incentive for our belief] and is also its Finisher [bringing it to maturity and perfection]. He, for the joy [of obtaining the prize] that was set before Him, endured the cross, despising and ignoring the shame, and is now seated at the right hand of the throne of God.*"[9]

ENDNOTES

1. Judges 4:6-7
2. Isaiah 61:10
3. "Princess," *Merriam-Webster.com*, Merriam-Webster Dictionary, Web. April 24, 2017.
4. Matthew 11:12
5. Daniel 11:32 KJV
6. Vallotton, Kris, "Before You Accept a Mantle, Understand What God Expects," *Charisma Magazine*, August 12, 2016, April 6, 2017, http://biblehub.com/str/hebrew/4150.htm.
7. Proverbs 20:15
8. Ephesians 1:11-14
9. Hebrews 12:2 AMP

Conclusion

RELEASING GOD'S GLORY

"Women are called to be a great power in the future."
Josephine Butler[1]

You Are Not an Ordinary Woman

Revival is coming to the Church and it is vital that we each walk in obedience to our call. We are in this battle together under the power and authority of the One who called us. We have inspirational examples of women who have gone before us and are among us today such as:

- Joan of Arc – a woman on the frontlines
- Perpetual – a martyr for her faith in the early church
- Sojourner Truth – a black woman leader in the antislavery movement
- Harriet Tubman – a black pioneer of the Underground Railroad

- Aimee Semple McPherson – a healing evangelist in the early 1920's
- Corrie Ten Boom – helped Jews escape the Nazi Holocaust
- Kathryn Kuhlman – powerful evangelist of the 20th century.

Today, you have women such as Patricia King, Cindy Jacobs, Barbara Yoder, Joan Hunter, Stacey Campbell, Lisa Bevere, Joyce Meyer, Arleen Westerhof, Royree Jensen, and many others impacting nations. Alongside them are women on the frontlines of business, family, media and other arenas contributing to the cause by fulfilling their call.

Let's posture our hearts to be well-pleasing to the Father, and take our place as a valuable, vital part of the the Body of Christ. Remember our battle is not against flesh and blood, but against things in the spiritual realm that fight for evil. We don't have to make the same mistake as Eve did. It's the time for God's daughters to rise and shine boldly for Him and be instrumental in His end time plan. We have a divine purpose and destiny and our future is bright.

The proclamation is going forth for God's daughters to arise and go forth to proclaim the Words He has spoken to you. There is an outpouring of His Spirit for the great awakening that is about to take place. He has placed a special message in the heart of His daughters. He is sending you forth with a message of redemption, reconciliation, and restoration. Abundant grace will be upon His daughters to testify powerfully of our Lord Jesus.

Psalm 68:11 says, "*The Lord gave the word: great was the company of those that published it.*" The word "*company*" comes from the Hebrew word *tsaba*, meaning "a mass of persons…organized for war (an army); a campaign: army, battle, company, host, service, soldiers."[2] You are a princess warrior empowered to live each day as a spirit-filled agent of

God who does the indescribable. You are also God's daughter with full rights to possess ALL of your spiritual inheritance in Christ.

Daughters of the King, do you know who you really are? Your Heavenly Father desires for you to step into you true identity, inheritance, and destiny. You have been equipped with beauty, intelligence, and wisdom. God is gently wooing His daughters back to His loving arms. Are you willing to pay the price for greater intimacy with him? God has a unique purpose for your life that only you, His royal daughter, can fulfill.

ENDNOTES

1. Pierce, Chuck, Josephine Butler, *God's Word to Women,* Web. April 6, 2017, https://godswordtowomen.org/chuck.htm.
2. "*Tsaba*" Strong's Hebrew Concordance 6635 *BibleHub.com,* Strong's Hebrew Dictionary, Web. April 24, 2017, http://biblehub.com/hebrew/6635.htm.

Meet the Author

Aleatha Francine Green is a minister, author, speaker, and founder of Beyond Church Walls Ministries. She is ordained through the Women in Ministry Network under the apostolic leadership of Patricia King.

Fran has served in various ministry and leadership roles within the local church for over two decades. She teaches, preaches, and offers counsel and so much more because of her strong desire to see God's healing and restoration reach women. Fran knows the power of this restoration process and that it is essential to embracing our identity in Christ and all that God desires to do for us.

Fran's heart is to see women arise and walk in their God-given destiny and inheritance in Christ. She is hungry for a move of God and determined to bring that move to this generation.

To stay connected with Fran, visit her website at BeyondChurchWalls.com, where she has additional media, articles, and resources.

Contact the Author:

Beyond Church Walls Ministries

Email: info@BeyondChurchWalls.com
Website: www.BeyondChurchWalls.com

SCRIPTURE COPYRIGHT INFORMATION

www.ingramcontent.com/pod-product-compliance
Lightning Source LLC
Chambersburg PA
CBHW051829090426
42736CB00011B/1711